Blue Ocean Faith

The vibrant connection to Jesus that
opens up insanely great possibilities
in a secularizing world—and might
kick off a new Jesus Movement

Dave Schmelzer

For more information and further discussion, visit

BlueOceanFaith.org

Cover art and design by
Rick Nease
www.RickNeaseArt.com

Author photo by Paul Choi.

Published By
Front Edge Publishing
42015 Ford Rd., Suite 234
Canton, Michigan, USA

For information about customized editions, bulk purchases or
permissions, contact Front Edge Publishing, LLC at
info@FrontEdgePublishing.com

Contents

Preface by Brian McLaren xii

Foreword by Peter Wallace xvii

Introduction by Adey Wassink xxiii

Preface: It's All About Connection xxxi

1. I'm Standing Behind "Insanely Great" 1

2. You Seriously Should be Solus Jesus 11

3. Centered-Set Faith is the Absolute Best 26

4. Childlike Faith Turns Out to Be the Only Road
   to Our Growth in God 46

5. Religious Squabbles Are the Worst
   (But There's an Antidote!) 70

6. Let's Defuse Religion's Seeds of Its Own Destruction . . 97

7. Engaging the Secular World Turns Out
   to be Super Fun 108

8. If You Have a Moment, Let's Kick Off
   a New Jesus Movement 131

Epilogue: You Want More Resources?
We've Got More Resources. 141

Appendix: Works Cited 142

For Grace, who has joyfully made sure
we don't deviate from this journey.
And for my dauntless fellow Blue Ocean pastors and leaders.
And for everyone who reads the thoughts in this book and
says, "Yes!"
Here's to a new Jesus Movement.

Praise for
Blue Ocean Faith

Blue Ocean Faith is a riveting book about an exciting new movement of churches emerging out of the ashes of American evangelicalism/fundamentalism. In vivid, readable prose filled with evocative real-life stories, Dave Schmelzer offers a deeply appealing understanding of Christian mission and church life that is comprehensively centered on the living Jesus and completely confident that Jesus draws people to himself if his followers will just not get in the way. *Blue Ocean Faith*, as a book, offers exceedingly important insights about Christian theology, scripture, mission, ethics, ecclesiology and public engagement, with profound critiques of dominant versions of Christianity on the American scene. This could be a charter document for a new kind of Jesus movement. Everyone should read it.

David P. Gushee, Distinguished University Professor of Christian Ethics and Director of the Center for Theology and Public Life at Mercer University. Author of *Changing Our Mind* and *A New Evangelical Manifesto: A Kingdom Vision for the Common Good.*

Blue Ocean Faith is one of those books that could actually change your way of thinking. It's not a simple "how-to" book, it's a rock-your-whole-world-and-everything-you-thought-you-knew sort of book. Words like "must read" get lost in the shuffle of book recommendations, but let me just say that I'll buy this one by the case and send it to all my friends. Read it.

Carl Medearis, author of *Speaking of Jesus* and *Adventures in Saying Yes*

~

I love Dave Schmelzer's voice: deceptively breezy (which makes for fun reading) but bristling with, well, brilliance.

Ken Wilson, author of *A Letter to My Congregation* and *Mystically Wired*

~

This book is full of breathtaking insights. It lays out an approach to faith that is so sane and life-giving. It has transformed my faith to be rational, spiritual, open-hearted, and grounded. I could not recommend it more. I believe this is the future of Christian faith.

Charles Park, Ph.D., Lead Pastor of The River Church, New York City.

Blue Ocean spirituality is among the most interesting approaches to faith out there, a striking and compelling combination of evangelical literalism and skeptical metaphor. This is a faith expression that manages to hold complexity and directness at the same time. *Blue Ocean Faith* is a wise, sensible guide towards how to think about and enact this new approach towards God.

Tanya Luhrmann is a psychological anthropologist at Stanford University and the author of *When God Talks Back: Understanding the American Evangelical Relationship with God.*

~

The Blue Ocean Faith theological distinctives that Dave fleshes out in this must-read book not only deepened my personal understanding of the gospel, but also greatly affected the way I pastor and lead. In a time and place when the gospel needs to have the dust brushed off of it, and when the way we do church must be re-imagined such that it compels people from all walks of life, the ideas and insights offered here will be like a cool drink of water on a hot muggy day.

Emily Swan, Co-Senior Pastor of Blue Ocean Faith, Ann Arbor

Preface by Brian McLaren

I MET DAVE Schmelzer many years ago when we both were pastors on the East Coast. He invited me to speak at his church. I believe it was May in Boston, and if I recall correctly, it either snowed or was insanely cold that weekend, or both. I remember two things about that weekend. The first was how much I liked Dave. I had been a college English teacher before becoming a pastor, and he had been a theater guy, so we clicked in that arts-and-humanities sort of way.

My second memory was that, although I was warmly received in Dave's church, some people there didn't click with me so much. Several people told me they thought I was coloring outside the lines of the Evangelical faith they considered normative.

I remember wondering: Would Dave get in trouble for inviting me? Did he struggle with the theological boundaries some of his parishioners were eager to maintain? What would become of him if he no longer fit?

I didn't hear from him for many years, and then I heard he had helped start something called Blue Ocean Faith. The name made perfect sense to me.

So many of us have found ourselves stuck in a religious suit of clothes that once fit but no longer does. Buttons pop and zippers malfunction and embarrassing tears happen. We worry about what will happen if we keep growing, asking honest questions, facing persistent doubts, and grappling with the unsolvable mysteries that life throws at us.

Dave has discovered what too few have discovered: that there is a tight-suit faith, and there is also a blue-ocean faith. One confines, one beckons. One limits, one liberates. One restrains, one expands.

I'm so glad that this book is available to introduce more people to Blue Ocean Faith. The book is beautifully written, from Adey Wassink's compelling introduction to Dave's shocking but important statistics in Chapter 1 ... from his honest confession in Chapter 2 to his wise insights about centered sets, childlike faith, religious squabbles, groupishness, and the joys of engaging our culture in succeeding chapters.

I'm especially thrilled with Dave's thoughts on a new Jesus Movement, because that, I think, is what our world needs most right now. True, lots of people still seem to find comfort, safety, and style in their tight-suit religion, but unprecedented numbers are done with it, and the kind of open-hearted, open-minded, open-armed faith this book describes is what their souls crave.

A couple years ago, I heard a former Islamic extremist say something profound. All of our world religions have, at times, been forces for peace, and all, at times, have been agents of hate and violence.

What our religions will be, he said, depends upon us, for, "A religion will be what its adherents make of it."

Blue Ocean Faith invites us to make of our faith something expansive, inclusive, deep, and beautiful. Launching out in search of a blue ocean faith might make some people nervous, but it will be to others good, good, good news.

Brian McLaren
Speaker, activist, and author of *The Great Spiritual Migration*

Foreword by Peter Wallace

AS THE PRODUCER and host of the weekly national radio program, "Day1," I have the honor and joy of working with scores of pastors, seminary professors, authors, and other preacher-types representing a very broad range of the Christian church.

During our program interviews, or even in our personal conversations, questions like these inevitably arise: "What is the future of the church? Where is it headed? Is Christianity dying? Or is it evolving, being transformed into something new?" And a concerned but usually hopeful conversation ensues.

Why these questions, and why now? Well, for many reasons. Among them, attendance numbers are continuously dwindling across the board. The church's influence on the culture is waning. Increasing numbers of people of all ages are simply turning away from all organized religion for all sorts of reasons.

So what is God up to anyway? And what should we do about it?

When we review church history, of course, it's evident that the church has always been evolving dramatically. The Reformation of 500 years ago resulted in major changes, without a doubt. But even over the past few decades the evolution seems to have accelerated once again. Perhaps even more than we realize.

This has certainly been true in my own life experience over six decades. I grew up as a preacher's kid during the heyday of the Protestant church—my late father was a respected and beloved Methodist pastor. In those days, the Methodist church and its mainline sibling denominations were massively influential.

The radio program I work with today started way back in 1945, when mainstream Christianity was a social force to be reckoned with. The organization built an enormous headquarters building with the largest movie/video production soundstage in the Southeast U.S., a sizable chapel with a pipe organ to record choral presentations, live services, and other programs, an audio recording studio used in the production of a variety of radio programs including ours (which was then called "The Protestant Hour"), and scads of offices and workrooms.

Today, the total square footage this same organization (which has also evolved greatly over the decades) leases on the ground floor of a church building would probably fit into the foyer space of that old, now demolished, mega-headquarters.

And yes, I'd say that is metaphorical.

Personally, I've evolved in my own faith over the years as well. I wandered from the Methodist church after college (though still quite friendly and at home with it), ended up at an independent seminary, meandered further among a few denominations and other expressions of church, and finally ended up in an Episcopal church some 25 years ago, and there I found my spiritual home. Eventually I became an ordained priest in what our presiding bishop, Michael Curry, calls the Episcopal Branch of the Jesus Movement.

The parish I now serve part-time is struggling as longtime members age or move—while at the same time it's growing rapidly as a new Hispanic outreach takes root as part of our parish's mission. Several churches in my diocese are thriving, while others are *this* close to shutting the doors for good. But it's not just the Episcopal Church struggling over what's happening and what to do about it. It's endemic.

The church is changing, whether we like it or not. But how is it changing? What is it becoming? Again I ask: What is God up to anyway? And what should we do about it?

"There has never been a more challenging time in [*fill in the blank*]. Everyone is scrambling to find the right way to connect to an audience that has fractured and fragmented to numerous different platforms."

That's how Edward Loh of *Motor Trend* magazine began his editor's note in an issue not long ago. He filled that blank with "automotive publishing." But how many times in recent days have we heard the same description attached to any number of formerly stalwart and influential societal and cultural institutions?

Print magazines hemorrhaging subscribers are scrambling to find ways to reinvent themselves, whether through tablet apps or websites or videos. But then, so are daily newspapers and traditional television networks, whose ratings even for the most popular shows fall far below what they were in the heyday of the last century, despite a much larger viewing population today.

An array of institutions that only a decade or two ago were considered pillars of American society seems to be collapsing around us. It may not be a new phenomenon—think of the glory days of the American railroads, for example—but it seems that more major institutions are declining at a more spectacular rate than at any time in memory.

In every case, naturally, those who are heavily invested in their particular declining institution are panicking, desperately attempting to figure out how to stem the unyielding tide, or else how to bail out and do something different. Some of the creative responses to this phenomenon are gaining some traction, but others are failing miserably.

And yet the reality some fail to recognize in this midst of this chaos is that *the need or function that all these declining institutions used to fulfill remains.* People have the same needs; they are simply choosing different ways, different platforms, to meet these needs.

For instance, people continue to want to access news and opinion, but fewer are willing to pay for and read a dead-tree newspaper to fulfill that need. And who needs an AM/FM radio when one can listen to whatever one wants whenever one wants via podcasts, Pandora, MP3 files or some other means?

Of course, the church is one of these major societal institutions that everyone includes in such doom-and-gloom scenarios. But I'm thinking maybe God knows what God is doing here. When the church was so huge and influential, was it authentically expressing and acting on the mission of Jesus Christ, or was it serving more as a social club or family habit?

Maybe people now are turning away from the fading show of inauthenticity and instead are yearning for the genuine.

Maybe people are craving real connection in their lives. A connection to their spiritual core, a relationship with the reality beyond themselves.

Maybe people really believe there is something more in life than the physical, and they are finding other ways and platforms to find it and satisfy their need.

Maybe people are seeking deeper connections with one another, with the communities in which they live, and even with the whole world.

Will the church offer them a way to find what they seek and fulfill what they yearn for?

For centuries, the church has been the primary delivery system for Christian faith and spirituality, but now people are finding what they're seeking in other expressions of the faith, individually and communally. So, like all the other struggling institutions, the church is "scrambling to find the right way to connect to an audience that has fractured and fragmented to numerous different platforms."

There are innumerable reasons why church attendance and involvement is declining. Many of them have to do with the abuse of power such structures can enable. Vast swaths of people are simply turning away from the judgmentalism and rigid views held by large portions of the church, and the rejection-with-a-smile of LGBTQ people. Much of the decline may be linked to certain political views some church groups espouse, or the spiritual and emotional damage that broken authority figures of organized religion have caused some people.

If it's not life giving and meaningful and authentic and truly loving, then what use is it?

Yet the need for spiritual connection and involvement remains. And always will.

So are there ways that "church" can regroup, can recast itself to fulfill this need in fresh, meaningful new ways?

Yes! And if you look around you, you will see a whole variety of ways this is happening today.

In this book you'll learn about what I believe is one of the most exciting and hopeful expressions of this new Jesus movement—a way to be the church, the Body of Christ, in this hurting world today. Authentically. Meaningfully. Actively. In lovingly welcoming and affirming ways.

It's Blue Ocean Faith.

I invite you to dive in.

The Rev. Peter M. Wallace is the executive producer and host of the Day1 radio program (Day1.org), author of *The Passionate Jesus* (Turner Publishing) and other books, and an Episcopal priest serving in the Diocese of Atlanta, Georgia.

Introduction by Adey Wassink

BLUE OCEAN FAITH has kept me sane.

Growing up Jewish, I went to Hebrew school every day, ate matzo and bologna sandwiches for lunch during Pesach, was Bas Mitzvahed at 13, and threw my sins into the Chicago River every Yom Kippur. But I never quite felt that these practices connected me to whoever, or whatever, they seemed to be all about. The disconnection between promise and reality was unsettling in a *this doesn't make sense* kind of way.

So one Rosh Hoshannah, I asked my friend Rhonna, "Do you think God is here?" We were both by then in our early 20s, attending yet another High Holiday service at the synagogue with our families, dressed nicely, listening to chanting and holy readings that were beautiful but that neither of us understood. My question had heightened urgency because my chaotic life needed help. The kind of urgency that a being called God might presumably provide.

But Rhonna looked pensive. "No," she said, "I don't think so."

So we went to the arboretum. The Morton Arboretum in Morton Grove, Chicago, being a sanctuary of sorts, seemed as likely a place as any to find God. Looking back, I'm pretty sure he was actually there. I felt something, a stirring that gave me hope that I was on the right track. Over the next six months, my search led not to Gaia, but frighteningly and miraculously for a Jew, to Jesus. He presented himself to me so compellingly and winningly and repeatedly that one night I said to him, "God, if you are Jesus, and you prove it to me tomorrow, I will give the rest of my life to serving you." He did, and I have.

My coming to Him worked, to a large degree, because it occurred in a community where the promise of his presence was fulfilled. Our church loved, valued and taught the Bible. As part of that, we believed that the experiences people had of God back then were what we could expect of him now. We prayed for God to come, and he came; we listened for his voice, and heard him speaking; we asked him to heal our bodies and our hearts and our relationships, and he did—not all the time, but enough to let us know that he was real and present and cared. The whole thing—the promise and the reality—held together, and I felt sane.

I dove into church. I joined, and eventually led, small groups. I forged a partnership between my church and a relief agency to help resettle Indochinese refugees. I taught classes, spoke at retreats and conferences, and before long was invited to join the pastoral staff. Somewhere in there I met and fell in love with a young man in my church who, thankfully, also fell in love with me. We got married, pursued Jesus together, served in the church, and had kids.

Then in 1996, Tom and I, and our five children, moved to Iowa City. We went, ostensibly, for Tom to pursue a career in scientific research. It was there that I again experienced a sanity-threatening disconnection between the promise and reality of the religious life to which Dave Schmelzer, Blue Ocean, and all the principles and values presented in this book turned out to be the answer.

Iowa City is home to the University of Iowa, with 30,000 students, a large teaching hospital, and an extensive biomedical research complex. Though encircled by cornfields and Amish horse-drawn carts, the city is a magnet for anyone with progressive, inquisitive, literary, scientific, artistic and/ or environmental inclinations, all energized by a bit of anti-establishment radicalism. As San Francisco is to California, or Austin to Texas, so Iowa City is to Iowa.

This presented a challenge for church. Tom and I checked out a lot of churches in town, many of which were awesome, and with which we, who by now had become longtime church attenders, might have been able to connect. However, when we'd bring neighbors or work friends, they'd be polite and nice, but refuse to come back.

We saw pretty quickly that most of what happened in church made no sense to them. These friends, who represented a huge swath of our community, were secular through and through, with either a remote or no meaningful experience of church. So the language, metaphors, principles and values—the *culture*—that came from our religious background and that packaged our connection to God was completely baffling to them. Here's the rub: Tom's a scientist, and I'm a hippie born one decade late. We loved the Iowa City vibe and felt that we'd come home. Which meant that as we saw church more and more through their eyes, we realized, startlingly, that a lot of it made no sense to us either! We had become them.

So we began doing church for them/us. Our planting team was me, Tom, our five children and a few hopeful stragglers. Our services were simple but tinged with adventure, and they apparently scratched a communal spiritual itch. We quickly outgrew our living room, then the subterranean laboratory classroom at Mercy Hospital, then the Robert A. Lee Recreation Center in downtown Iowa City, arriving not too long ago in the lovely space we now inhabit, called Sanctuary.

Our congregants were eclectic. Joining us was Geoff, who called himself a ZenJewtheran, George, a Mennonite pastor who'd been fired for marrying those who'd been divorced and welcoming those who were LGBTQ, our genetics grad student Dani who needed to know that we weren't dismissive of evolution, and Harmony, hungry for God, willing to connect to him through Jesus, but completely unfamiliar with even the concept of church.

With these people, we began asking questions that challenged dearly held traditional notions of God. Is His welcome more open than ours? What does it mean that His voice from the Bible comes through humans? Does He care about whales even more than Greenpeace? Is He excited, rather than threatened, by science? Is He less preoccupied than us with misbehavior?

These were good questions, but wow, did they provoke anxiety for an eager-to-please-God person who had inhabited a theologically and experientially conservative Christian tradition for 20 years. What if we weren't supposed to ask these questions? Or worse, what if our answers came out wrong? Our culturally secular church was, at this point, still ensconced in the denomination in which I'd come to faith. Though wonderful for my spiritual formation, they viewed such questions with disdain. Hence my craziness. In our church in Iowa City I felt connected to Jesus, happy, and intellectually alive. When I engaged with our broader church movement, I felt heretical, uncentered and anxious.

So when I first heard Dave speak, my heart started beating fast. It was at a Midwest regional meeting of our church denomination, and I texted Tom, who was holding down the fort at home, "I think we've found a friend!" Dave talked about how a centered, rather than bounded-set model, better described what church structure ought to be. He described a stage theory of spiritual development that was helpful for understanding both personal and spiritual growth, and why Christian denominations squabble so much. He presented a compelling rationale for a warm and amicable, rather than aloof and critical, engagement with secular culture.

Normally, I can't remember what I had for breakfast or my kids's names, but though this meeting occurred more than a decade ago, I still remember it vividly. With each word I'd think, "That's what we've been asking! That's what we've been thinking!" Dave was expounding with confidence and depth the nascent thoughts that we had only tenuously begun to consider.

Less than a year later we attended the first meeting of what would become the Blue Ocean Church Network. About 20 of us drew up folding chairs to rickety tables in the basement of the Boston church that Dave then led. We shared together how our concepts of God had been shaped by the cultural waters, in which we now happily swam. We talked for hours about the relevance of Jesus for our non-religious and secular, but spiritually interested friends.

I was blown away when I saw how Dave and his Boston crew had taken these thoughts and run with them. Thinkers often flounder when translating Grand Ideas into real life practices. However, beyond adding theological depth, Dave and his crew had begun to operationalize the welcome of Jesus towards secular culture into concrete, tested, transferrable *and successful* practices. The Seek course for exploring Jesus and faith, the Lenten Leap of Faith exercise, and the prayer discipline of praying for your six. These were spiritual practices that resonated with contemporary life through ordinary, non-churchy language and that anyone, from within themselves, could easily try out.

Over the ensuing years, we formed a deep partnership with Dave and our other Blue Ocean friends. We participated in elaborating the values and principles laid out in this book. By the time we left our previous denomination to dive deep into the Blue Ocean, we felt unadulterated joy. Jesus had helped us uncover a treasure in a field that felt worth selling everything for. We also felt sane, because the desire of God to be present in the world we inhabited was once again being actualized.

Tom's *Aha* moment came after giving a talk on Darwin and Jesus at a Blue Ocean conference in Ann Arbor, Michigan. "They liked it!" he said, skipping down the sidewalk. "No one was worried or suspicious because I'm a scientist asking questions—without anything even approaching an answer—about how Jesus interacts with evolution. I'd rather be free like this with ten people than trapped in whatever it was we were doing before with a million!"

My moment came in a conversation with Ryan. As part of our church's dive into Blue Ocean, we had embraced full welcoming and inclusion for LGBTQ individuals. Ryan, who lived in a city two hours away, called me saying that he had just told his youth pastor that his gender identification was ambiguous. Though biologically male, Ryan told his pastor that when filling out forms, if he had to check either the M box for male or the F box for female, he was stuck because he was the air outside the boxes.

I met Ryan for coffee and my first question was how he got my name. He told me that his pastor, in explaining why Ryan needed to step down from the worship team and maybe take a break from church while he sorted things out, had heard about a nice woman pastor in Iowa City with a church where anyone was welcome. "Hooray for us!" I thought.

Ryan was super-likable. He told me his story, which was complicated, fraught and often stretched the limits of words. He used lots of pictures and metaphors to help me understand. He was often tearful.

My job, now swimming in the centered-set reality of the Blue Ocean, was simple here: point Ryan to Jesus, walk with Ryan to Jesus, remove obstacles between Ryan and Jesus, connect Ryan to Jesus, knowing that Jesus would be waiting, joyful and welcome to receive him. He had a two-hour commute to our church, so Ryan worshiped with us only for a season. I think his experience of us was good; I know he changed me forever.

Not long ago, a small group of us symbolized our commitment to the adventure that has become Blue Ocean Faith by reenacting, in a Lower West Side Manhattan apartment, crossing of water, an event through which God repeatedly leads the Israelites out of an old identity into something new. Read on to hear what has compelled me and my husband and our wonderful faith community here in the awesome state of Iowa to join in that adventure.

Adey Wassink
Sanctuary Church
Iowa City, IA

Preface: It's All About Connection

I WAS LATE to the party in hearing about Wiz Khalifa and Charlie Puth's "See You Again," from the soundtrack to *Furious 7*. It's a big party. The video of the song is, as I write this, the fifth most-viewed video ever on YouTube.[1] It was number one on the Billboard Hot 100 for 12 straight weeks, tied for the longest run for a rap song ever. It has the Spotify record for most-streamed song in one day, and has the record in 26 countries for most-streamed song in a week.

I gave it a listen this morning and choked up about three chords in. Evidently the entire world except me knows that it was written as a tribute to the late Paul Walker. "It's been a long day without you, my friend/ And I'll tell you all about it when I see you again." Well, I had a friend as close as a brother who died young and, as I listened, my emotions about him

1 As of today: 1.61 billion views. It was the first rap video to cross a billion views and was the third-fastest to a billion, after "Gangnam Style" and Adele's "Hello." I mean, the Chipmunks cover of it has ten million views.

were right there. Clearly, I'm not the only one who chokes up about lost friends upon hearing this song, but I realized my emotions weren't just about my friend. As I listened, I was getting weepy about the *prospect* of being separated from people I love.

The video is great too, beautiful, evocative and somber, ending with a sequence from the movie in which Vin Diesel's character and his "brother," Paul Walker's character, race each other one last time until they hit a fork in the road and one car goes one way and one goes the other. *The Fast and Furious* movies are remarkable pictures of multi-racial bonding which, as many people have noted, taps into a cultural fantasy. We want to believe we're not Balkanized into ghettos of our own race and class, that we can connect with people not like us. In the video, the white, pompadoured, looks-about-14-years-old Charlie Puth croons as the wiry, African American Wiz Khalifa raps. Would these guys ever hang out together? I don't know, but they sure make beautiful music together.

After hearing the song, I found myself marveling that something so earnest was so popular. The song and the video are heartfelt rather than cool. Maybe responding to this song is hardwired into all of us. We know that we're going to die, that we'll have people leave us behind on our journey, and that someday we'll leave others behind. And we choke up.

About a year ago, my wife Grace and I were having drinks with three visiting couples who are the kind of friends who might someday choke us up as we listen to "See You Again." Grace and I live in California, and we were sitting outdoors on a fall night on a lovely, trendy patio with potted trees, lattices and little, white lights. All of us have reflective temperaments and we were trying to pin down what had been so transformative for us when it came to the things about God that we were learning. Charles was the one who nailed it. "It's that it's all about connection," he said. "We think we want answers in life. We want to know why we have pain, just like Job did. But, like Job discovered when he finally got to talk with God face to face, we discover that it's not about answers and we don't need them. We need connection."

This got a heartfelt agreement. Did religion that didn't work so well for us encourage *disconnection*?

Mostly, yes.

"Mostly" in that one of the great gifts of any church, whatever it teaches, is that churches tend to connect people, often the kinds of people who would never meet apart from that setting. Connection is embedded right into the endeavor. But many churches we'd experienced were dominated by drawing lines between good people and bad people and good behavior and bad behavior. The truths taught there were often abstractions, and abstractions seem to be better at dividing people, rather than gathering people in.

But the God we'd all discovered over many years was not abstract, but was very concrete in his[2] connection with us. We found ourselves talking about passages like Ephesians 2:15-17,[3] where Paul pitched that the big miracle Jesus brought was breaking down disconnection in ways that were inconceivable before him. We remembered C.S. Lewis's memorable appeal

---

2 I haven't solved the problem of using pronouns in talking about God. I mean we know from Genesis 1:27 that God isn't male, right? "So God created mankind in his own image,/ in the image of God he created them;/ male and female he created them." Yet, in this very verse we get "his" and "he," which does tend to be the dominant image in the rest of the Bible, perhaps understandable in a patriarchal society. One friend strongly urged me to avoid pronouns altogether and always call God "God," but that seems awkward. Interspersing "she" seems distracting. So I might be wrong in this, but be ye warned: there will be some "hes" and "hims" that refer to God in what follows. I'm duly sheepish about it.

3 "His purpose was to create in himself one new humanity out of the two, thus making peace, and in one body to reconcile both of them to God through the cross, by which he put to death their hostility. He came and preached peace to you who were far away and peace to those who were near."

in *The Great Divorce* that hell was ever-expanding alienation. We talked about the remarkable conclusion of Harvard's 75-year, $25 million study of what makes for long-range happiness: "Happiness is love. Full stop."[4] We wondered if this was why Congress's approval rating was so low (under 10% at that point, the worst in the history of polling)—while some small constituencies felt an ever-growing need for the kind of purity that would require shaming and separating from the vast majority of Americans (who were infidels), it seemed that most poll respondents dreamed of a government that would connect us, rather than drive us apart. Yet, they despaired that it was possible, and like Paul in Ephesians, they thought it would take a miracle.

We reflected that, in our own lives, this miraculous connection had come in several different spheres: connection to God, but also connection to other people, even connection to our cities. We also talked a fair amount about experiencing a kind of supernatural connection to ourselves, and that our customarily negative self-talk and separation from our full emotional life had seen a lot of transformation. We marveled again that, alongside our churchgoing friends, we'd all been learning more and more about what a connected faith in Jesus actually looks like. For some of us, this had taken a lot of unlearning! But, one of the surprising good outcomes of this was discovering how many previously non-churchgoing people were drawn to this, couldn't believe they'd stumbled upon this amazing thing they had no idea was possible.

So, we toasted, here's to connection! Here's to discovering and maybe helping a few others discover the God who's so motivated to pull off this miracle in us!

And when one of us leaves this earth behind, while it may be a long day without our friend, with this God we'll look forward to telling them all about it when we see them again.

---

4 I write about the study for the meaning-of-life website, Horatio (which I also edit). http://www.hellohoratio.com/articles/spirituality/harvard-has-figured-out-secret-happiness

I'm Standing Behind "Insanely Great"

A depressing article cheers me up.

I'VE JUST BEEN so happy today.

Now—happily!—I'm at a point where that's been true more than it has ever been in my adult life—which will become part of our story. A key prod to today's particular happiness is that a friend sent me a GQ article about a booming, hip church.[5] It was written by a sympathetic, secular Jewish woman who marveled at the genuinely amazing aspects of this hot church— the dynamic worship and the sincere faith, among other things. She also marveled less positively about other aspects of the church's culture—largely how the pastor seemed so tortured as he explained to her why he and their church needs to draw lines against a lot of people, certainly gay people (which to him goes without saying) but also secular, godless people in general. This very hip, sincere pastor (who, the author points out, seems to lead a congregation entirely of transplants from other churches) just seemed so miserable at this point of the conversation.

It was a misery I felt sympathy with.

So, as I've talked about in another book,[6] I entered faith in Jesus from atheism (or maybe hard agnosticism; it's hard to be sure these years later, though I did spend years as an

---

5 http://www.gq.com/story/inside-hillsong-church-of-justin-bieber-kevin-durant?mbid=social_twitter

6 *Not the Religious Type: Confessions of a Turncoat Atheist* (Tyndale 2008)

amateur, anti-God debater). While the suburb I grew up in was largely conservative and churchgoing, I was a culturally-engaged skeptic and, in my adult life, I hadn't lived among those conservative churchgoers. My college friends and my neighbors in San Francisco's Mission District were secular. I was a *New York Times* reader and a playwright whose hero was George Bernard Shaw, one of the great modern atheist debaters.

It was from that culture that I entered a three decade sojourn into evangelicalism. After having what felt like a dramatic encounter with this God, who seemed entirely eager to get my attention, and after a two-year comparative religion study-fest, I was convinced that my story had to be about Jesus. I tried to find people who could help me understand the story I appeared to have entered. I found an awesome campus evangelical group that had high faith and a passion for studying the Bible. The churches that believed in this transcendent, communicative, powerful God I'd discovered were evangelical or evangelical/charismatic. After a couple of years working to start a ministry to kids in a high-crime neighborhood, I went to the country's largest evangelical seminary to learn more about this faith I'd stumbled into. And then, after a decade working as a playwright (and working the day jobs that went along with that), my wife and I joined some friends hoping to start a church across the country in Cambridge, Massachusetts, and I spent the next eighteen or so years as a pastor.

I loved it, despite my surprise at having found my way into that line of work at all. I said repeatedly that I didn't know anyone—doing pastor work or otherwise—who'd found a better gig than I had. The church boomed, becoming Cambridge's largest Protestant church, and one filled with a remarkably high number of attendees who hadn't previously attended any church. We got some press attention and I got invited into some fun and unexpected gigs, such as moderating faith/atheism debates at Harvard and speaking in all sorts of interesting settings, like at joint gatherings between Christian and atheist clubs. We got a whole lot of interest from other churches who wanted to learn the secrets of our success in a place with a churchgoing rate that was among the lowest in America. It's hard to express how lucky—or blessed—I felt to have fallen so unexpectedly into that wonderful opportunity.

There is a "that said."

Which is that, for all the really impressive things I learned through the years in these church settings, there was one noteworthy dark side—which I was reminded of in the article my friend sent me today. I tell a story in *Not the Religious Type* about a conversation which sums this up for me. A pastor friend—who was on the verge of trying another line of work—said nice things about how much he enjoyed my sermons, which he found to be so positive and encouraging. But he wondered what the settings were in which I talked with people about "the bad news." Remembering that "gospel" means "good news," I wasn't sure I was following him. He said, "The bad news! The fine print!" As we talked, it seemed to me that he meant several things by this. "The bad news" was that, while, certainly, it was awesome to follow Jesus, it also meant we had to change our ways, to jettison that drug habit or whatever our vice was. It also meant that we had to learn things that, if not learned, could cause our friends and neighbors (and maybe us) to be sent to hell. That felt pressurized.

I said that I didn't believe in any bad news as we followed Jesus, that "gospel" was the right word to describe what we'd gotten ourselves into, that the main reason to jettison a heroin habit was because very few people grew up dreaming of having a heroin habit. Yes, there was certainly suffering and pain and rejection that we'd go through in life, but there was nothing bad at all about following Jesus. In my experience, that was all upside.

Still, his characterization of "the bad news" has stuck with me. This bad news is at the heart of the misery that the sincere pastor in the GQ article describes. The secular Jewish writer really liked the church except for that! She talked at the end about how she misses being there, but she also details how she could never join a church that was so focused on who to exclude, and has such misery-inducing elements to its creed.

What made me so happy today was realizing I wasn't a part of that world anymore. Free at last! It's been quite a rush these last few hours.

Jettisoning the bad news does great things for two groups of people: (A) non-churchgoers and (B) churchgoers.

We got some attention in Cambridge because hundreds and hundreds of previously non-churchgoing people, many of them working at hoity-toity places like Harvard, (though many also living in nearby housing projects) came to us looking for connection to Jesus and ended up enthusiastically finding that connection. What, we were asked many times, was our secret? I believe it ties into this conversation about the necessity, or lack thereof, of embracing the bad news.

Some of our friends who were committed to the bad-news parts of the gospel had concerns. Would, for instance, this way of following Jesus lead to a lack of rigor in one's faith? I suppose it's possible. However, our experience is that it was just the reverse. Person after person took consequential risks of faith, congregational giving was far higher than in even the strongest comparable churches, working among at-risk communities happened more than at any other church in town, and intellectual engagement with faith soared among some very educated people.

As we drew interest from around the world, we got together to compare notes with a few friends who pastored churches in similarly non-churchgoing settings. Their advice was to do what pastors who feel like they're onto something interesting usually do: throw a conference. There was a lot of interest!

With only word-of-mouth advertising, people came from 25 states. From South Africa. From Japan.

We learned something really important at that first conference that was related to this good news/bad news conversation. About half of the people seemed to tune into what we were talking about, but the other half really, really didn't. Here was the key issue. The ones who ended up frustrated with us had come looking for tactics. If we were the hot church-people who knew how to draw secular people into our church, well, what were our tactics to accomplish such a thing?

Oh, we realized, what a helpful question! It validated hosting such conversations after all! Our answer: We didn't have any tactics. We had a mindset. But no tactics.

Some people asked, "I mean, surely you have *some* tactics to offer! If only to help us understand what it's like to be the cool, hip thing!" We had an obvious answer to that one. Just look at us. We're not cool and hip.

That did get nods.

In fact, we continued, focusing on being cool and hip would actually work against what we're trying to do (except for our rare friends who were just naturally cool and hip, in which case, hey, let your light so shine!). No, seriously, it was a mindset. In fact, if anyone needed to convert for this to "work," it was us churchgoers.

With some of our attendees, this turned out to be a disappointing answer, to say the least. One man shouted a speaker down from the crowd. The whole thing ended up being boisterous in the way that a political convention ends up having picketers.

What we discovered in these conversations is at the heart of this book. It's a kind of living, relational connection to Jesus that seems to answer deep cravings both from people who'd never imagined they'd be interested in Jesus, as well as from longtime churchgoers. We discovered that—who knew?— what people seemed to want most was a rich connection to

Jesus! And, from that, a rich connection to everything else, but not a connection based on truisms but on something a lot more living than that. Tactics are about finding clever and ever-changing ways to take "them" and make them "us." Our ever-growing discovery was that all the power came from continually understanding more and more about what exactly God's offer to any of us actually is. While, okay, we actually do have a tactic here or there (which only become meaningful when this mindset is in place; that said, I wrote a whole book about them, which you can find for free at blueoceanfaith. org), the rest of this book will do its best to flesh out this transforming mindset.

For many years in our congregation I led a popular course, developed in Great Britain, for people who were exploring faith. This British course has had lots of success in many countries. I liked it fine, and we saw people experience Jesus out of it. However, we heard a litany of low-level complaints each time we ran it. The complaints came to a head with one conversation I had with a local college dean. "Look," he said, "I spend my whole day arguing. I'm good at it. But I don't actually believe in arguing, because what I've learned is that arguments get won by the best arguer, not necessarily by the best argument. And what you're giving me with this course is a lot of arguments about God. First off, it's all I can do not to engage and argue back. And I'm confident that, if I did, I'd—how do I put this nicely?—decimate you. But what's the point? Because I've come to your course because you strike me as someone who could help me discover whether or not there's a God who could make a real difference in my life. So I would regard it as hospitable on your part if you'd, rather than trotting out all these arguments about things that I guess you think are related to this God, instead would just coach me into discovering this God for myself. If you do, well then I guess you win. If you don't, I guess you lose. But, either way, I'd have a lot better experience." From that, we created a whole new course[7] and realized, yet again, that the best upside of getting to know God was, well, getting to know God.

We found ourselves having increasingly robust conversations with a lot of churches in very non-churchgoing parts of the world. This was the consistent feedback we were getting: their best sales-pitch to everyone, non-churchgoers and churchgoers alike, was that the actual, living, communicative Jesus was awesome. "There was no shadow of turning in him"[8]—it was all good news. It was a basic, but notably powerful pitch.

In our first conference, that pitch also began to generate controversy.

While, yes, certainly Jesus was wonderful, wasn't this Jesus we were talking about kind of … subjective? If everything boiled down to connection, who was to say whether the connection that you or I claimed to be experiencing was the real deal? And they had a point: relationships, indeed, were pretty subjective. They were experienced by the actual people inside of them.

We really should be talking about this.

I'd love to run some related statistics by you.

A 2008 survey[9] by the Pew Forum on Religion and Public Life (at that point the largest such survey yet conducted, with over 36,000 adult participants) told us that about a quarter of Americans change the faith of their upbringing.[10] The religious demographic benefiting the most from this religious churn

---

7 It's called Seek. You can learn more at BlueOceanFaith.org.

8 James 1:17

9 http://www.pewtrusts.org/en/research-and-analysis/ reports/2008/02/25/us-religious-landscape-survey-religious-affiliation

10 I'm adapting this discussion from the free, online book that I mentioned a moment ago. It's called *Blue Ocean Churches: Thriving Congregations in a Changing World,* and it's a how-to manual for setting up a Blue Ocean Church. It's mildly out-of-date now—time moving on as it does. But if you're looking for tips along these lines,

are those who claim no religious affiliation. They've since been dubbed the "nones." The people moving into that category outnumbered those moving out of it by a three-to-one margin. The nones were the only "religious" (as it were) affiliation to gain in all 50 states in their comparative surveying.

Christine Wicker, one-time religious reporter for the *Dallas Morning News* has compiled related information in her book, *The Fall of the Evangelical Nation: The Surprising Crisis Inside the Church*. Here are some bullet points that get my attention:

- Outside of the South, Churches of Christ lose 80 percent of the kids in their youth groups once the kids graduate high school.

- Of those who leave, only 12 percent return once they marry and have kids of their own.

- Southern Baptists estimate that 88 percent of their kids leave church after high school.

- Josh McDowell Ministries, a group that focuses on youth, reports that 94 percent of high school graduates leave the faith within two years.[11]

Let's just let that soak in for a minute: *94%*! As if pretty much *all* youth, in many large church settings, leave faith when they leave home!

This matches up with what we saw in Boston. Dozens of universities are within a ten mile radius of the church (the closest and the one we had most contact with being Harvard) and the student population in Greater Boston during the school year is about 250,000. The total involvement among all campus ministries (apart from Christian colleges) in 2008 numbered about 2,000 students, or less than one percent. This does catch one's attention after having read the Gallup organization tells us that, nationwide, *35% of these kids were*

this will certainly give you the spirit of the enterprise. You can get it at http://blueoceanfaith.org/.

11 Christine Wicker, *The Fall of the Evangelical Nation: The Surprising Crisis Inside the Church* (HarperOne, 2008), p. 124.

churchgoers on any given week before they showed up to their campus.

Younger Westerners are flooding out of churches. These numbers also match up with surveying that the Barna group was doing, which closes with this arresting observation.

"The vast majority of (secular people) don't need to hear the Good News. They have been exposed to Christianity in an astonishing number of ways, and that's exactly why they're rejecting it. They react negatively to our 'swagger', how we go about things, and the sense of self-importance we project." They quote one outsider as saying, "Most people I meet assume that Christian means very conservative, entrenched in their thinking, antigay, antichoice, angry, violent, illogical, empire builders; they want to convert everyone, and they generally cannot live peacefully with anyone who doesn't believe what they believe."[12]

In 2015, the Pew folks released an update.[13] Among the noteworthy statistics were that the Christian share of the population had fallen from 78.4% in 2008 to 70.6%, or one percentage point per year since the last survey.[14] The share of nones rose approximately seven percent, from 16.1% to 22.8%. In eight years. The trends, which were already quite striking in 2008, are accelerating.

My friends and I think about this stuff a lot. Maybe improved tactics will reverse these trends. But our experience

---

12 Quoted in Wicker, p. 189.

13 http://www.pewforum.org/2015/05/12/americas-changing-religious-landscape/

14 The bulk of this decline came among mainline and Catholic Christians, though evangelicals also declined 1% (while seeing some growth in raw numbers, just not enough to keep up with population growth). That said, David Putnam and Robert Campbell, in their magisterial *American Grace: How Religion Divides and Unites Us* (Simon & Schuster, 2012) point out that evangelicalism declined each year from 1992 to 2010 after having crested in the 1980s in the Reagan years.

has been that, given that all people are created to experience the good news that Jesus brings (or so we stipulate), these mindset questions are far more promising.

From conversation among a lot of churches has come a new network of churches dedicated entirely to this exploration. "Blue Ocean" has become the descriptor of these churches— and this point of view—both because these churches tend to "fish where other churches don't fish"[15] and because it's the blue oceans that connect all people. While the network is still small, maybe in the spirit of the mustard seed that Jesus talks about, this small band has the enthusiasm of people who feel like they're in on something big.

But what if the bad news is the real deal? Can we really just blow it off?

Talking about the ins and outs of that question is at the heart of the rest of this book. For now let me just foreshadow where we're headed by saying that all this has changed my life. It by no means is the only word on faith in Jesus. God's reality does turn out to be quite large, as we'll talk about.

But, in my experience, this is an insanely great starting point.

---

15 This take on "Blue Ocean" comes from the awesome Blue Ocean business strategy people (https://www.blueoceanstrategy.com/).

2

You Seriously Should be Solus Jesus

"What does it mean to follow Jesus?" turned out to be a surprisingly hard question.

AGAIN, AS AN atheist debater, I had a powerful, ongoing encounter with a God who seemed eager to get my attention. Two years of studying the religious options convinced me that this sort of living, personal, loving, communicating God could only be explained by Jesus, and that epiphany has paid off remarkably in the years since. My temperament always wants more perspective on anything that matters. Trying, over a few decades, to hunt down this kind of perspective about following Jesus has played out in two noteworthy ways.

One is intellectual.

When I realized that I'd been wrong in my years of atheist debating, I was eager to be taught by the Christians, by the experts, by the people who'd mastered this way of living with Jesus. I got a graduate degree in theology. I read the classic thinkers about Jesus from most centuries since Jesus' life. I read just about any current book that anyone I knew liked. I interviewed pastors and older Christians. I practiced every prayer practice anyone ever taught me. I spent two years living among the poor in the town with the highest murder-per-capita rate in the country. I read the Bible daily for decades. All of that led me to a helpful conclusion that had staying power.

Nobody has figured this out. No one. Nobody.

That guru of how-to-follow-Jesus doesn't exist.

Of course that doesn't mean that no one has any insights about Jesus! I'm like Pavlov's dogs to this day. Whenever anybody rings the bell by telling me how terrific some thinker about Jesus is, I salivate by reflexively dialing up my Amazon account and buying that book before the conversation's done. Just this week, someone favorably mentioned an obscure theological book from a couple of decades back. When he casually referenced it ten minutes later and started summarizing the small point that had most helped him, I said, "Oh, I've already ordered it. I'll read the whole thing and get back to you."

But when I started going to churches, many pastors would speak with confidence that "the Bible said 'x.'" The world they painted was one where, sooner or later, with the right amount of study and spiritual practice, one would master this thing called "biblical Christianity." They said that since the Bible was by and large clear, "becoming biblical" was mostly a matter of honest labor.

It took me decades of this labor before I finally called the fight. What I'd been told in all those churches could now persuasively be called false.

It now seemed clear to me that the authorities these pastors looked to were mostly modern, confident scholars who were asking only narrow questions, but who often claimed to be asking vast questions. To my just-learning-this-stuff eyes, they appeared to have limited emotional maturity. It wasn't that these writers didn't say anything worth saying! They would each have an insight or two very worth considering, but it seemed to me that the pastors who made these men their gurus (always men, in these cases) also often demonstrated a narrow range of emotional and spiritual maturity. Some of them grew large churches, but the appeal of their churches struck novice-Dave as that of having a strong, if perhaps shallow leader telling congregants what's what.

When I moved on to thinkers about Jesus who seemed to have great depth, these thinkers still had their feet of clay.

Augustine gave us the Confessions at the same time as he was
persecuting his religious opponents and unleashing a theology
of sexuality, which most of my friends regard as having
damaged its adherents ever since. Calvin gave us the Institutes
while he was putting his opponents to death and working to
create an ideal, godly city which, to the modern reader, looks
a lot like a city under Sharia Law. The greatest pleasures that
Luther offers my friends who read him seem to be his robust
insults towards his opponents. Even the favorite thinker of
many late-twentieth-century western Christians, C.S. Lewis,
seemed only to be attempting a modest project: to mount a
defense of the reasonableness of Christianity against attacks
on it from the secular world of his day.

Again, it's not that there were no insights to be found in
these people![16] But they strike me as the insights of a delightful
thrift store. As we dig through the bin in the far corner, we
discover how so and so prayed the scriptures. As we dig
through the bin near the register, we discover so and so's
view of 1 Corinthians 14—wow, that's interesting stuff! As we
rummage through the pile of shirts, we see how someone lived
out their understanding of Jesus' care for the poor.

So the first consequence of decades of playing out my drive
for perspective about following Jesus was realizing that, unless
I missed it, no one has that perspective, that there's no answer
to that question. Maybe that's not entirely bad news. I think of
the exchange Jesus had with the Pharisees in John 9.

---

16 Or in the many great women who've written on faith. One
difference with them is that very few have attempted to set up entire
systems the way the men above did.

"Jesus said, 'For judgment I have come into this world, so that the blind will see and those who see will become blind.' Some Pharisees who were with him heard him say this and asked, 'What? Are we blind too?' Jesus said, 'If you were blind, you would not be guilty of sin; but now that you claim you can see, your guilt remains.'"[17]

Maybe our mistake all along has been claiming that we can see. Maybe Jesus has another plan in mind to accomplish what he has in mind that doesn't involve us insisting upon a (facile?) "biblical Christianity."

The second consequence isn't intellectual. It's emotional.

And that's that the effort itself has a surprising payoff, if I go about it by staying in close contact with Jesus. The downside of all my need for perspective is some level of isolation. But the more I connected with Jesus, the more I found myself connected not just to God, but also to my world and myself. I still lacked my big-picture "answer," but this connection was a very nice gift for someone like me. Maybe this was also predicted in John's Gospel, as Jesus talked about the whole ballgame involving staying connected to him, like branches stay connected to a vine.[18]

Those two consequences lead into what have become the six distinctives of Blue Ocean, which try to sort out the strange discovery I and many of my friends made.[19] Why is it that a certain sort of "figuring things out about life with Jesus" didn't seem to be as helpful as it sometimes claimed to be, while a different sort of ever-maturing connection with Jesus did seem so powerful? Are there ways to craft an experience of faith that will better chart a course towards the good outcome?

---

17 *Vv. 39-41*

18 John 15:4

19 These distinctives exist in time, so they might well change! But let's revel in the spirit of Zechariah 4:10 and "not despise the day of small beginnings."

The six distinctives of Blue Ocean

1. Our primary framework is SOLUS JESUS.
2. Our primary metaphor is CENTERED-SET.
3. Our approach to spiritual development is CHILDLIKE FAITH.
4. Our approach to controversial issues is THIRD WAY.
5. Our approach to other churches is ECUMENICAL.
6. Our approach to secular culture is JOYFUL ENGAGEMENT.

Sola scriptura was astounding and needed, but now it's become the problem.

This ties into my first discovery.

Protestantism was created by a few "solas" (meaning "alone"). Perhaps the most meaningful and lasting of them to our Lutheran friends would be "sola fide," "by faith alone." Maybe you've heard the phrase "justification by faith" rather than by "works," by good things that we do. That was a big point of how Lutheranism (and Protestantism) separated from Rome.

But our evangelical friends have given even more attention to another of the solas—"sola scriptura" or "scripture alone." The problem it was trying to solve was figuring out who had the authority to say what God's will was. Roman Catholicism had answered that by pointing out that Jesus gave Peter the keys to his church, and that Peter then passed them on to leaders in his church. So the Pope and his leaders were the final authority. By Luther's day, they were obviously corrupt, so Luther proposed a new authority that would not have been possible until that point in history. He and his fellow reformers proposed that the authority didn't sit with any fallible human beings, but with the holy and unchanging words of God in the Bible. Sola scriptura. That spurred a massive literacy campaign in Europe. The printing press was just coming into play, which soon made it at least theoretically possible for a literate person to read the Bible for him or herself.[20] The challenge from Rome was quick. Fine, they said, let's say, following your logic, that the scriptures are the authority. Who has the right or the ability to interpret them? The answer was novel: the scriptures were "clear" in all essential matters. Any reader of good will would, as my early pastors preached so aggressively, understand them just fine if they put in a minimum of work.

We've already established that I've found that to be a falsehood, but let's get back to that later.

First, let's celebrate sola scriptura for a moment.

Again, it created widespread literacy as we experience it today.

Also, Christians in the evangelical tradition now routinely get told that daily Bible reading is the key to their hope of growth in Jesus. I think that has downsides (more on that in a moment), but I say that as a massive beneficiary. Starting to follow Jesus in college, I was in many hours of group Bible study each week in my campus fellowship, along with my highly encouraged personal daily Bible reading. That luxurious experience of studying the Bible with (and without) friends was bonding, encouraging, motivating, informative and among the best parts of my college life. It lived up to its billing as something that shaped me and shaped my future. As someone with a literary bent, it captured my imagination. I was a playwright for years in secular settings and the biblical story informed everything I wrote, as it does for every earnest evangelical. I dreamed for years of writing the first great drama about Paul. My family and I, like all families and individuals, have gone through hardship and betrayal and anxiety. All that Bible reading that Grace and I did over all those years was crucial in directing us how to navigate those challenges and discouragements and still end up close to a

---

20 In practice, of course, it was mostly impossible for a few centuries afterward.

good God who loves us. The heritage of sola scriptura has been among the great gifts I've gotten.

But there are cracks in the armor.

Some of the cracks are, intriguingly, biblical cracks. Neither Jesus, nor Paul, nor Peter were sola scriptura people. Actually, their opponents better fit that description. Their opponents were the ones who were "serious about the Bible." Jesus, Peter and Paul were the ones who scandalized them by abandoning the "clear" teachings. Jesus picked grain on the Sabbath and hugged lepers. Peter went into the home of a Gentile despite the quite clear biblical prohibitions against it. Paul kept getting himself jailed and nearly killed by his constant tweaks to the serious Bible people of his day. Jesus, Peter and Paul seemed scandalously "free" to the sola scriptura people.

Some of the cracks are practical. Sola scriptura, it turns out, can't actually give life. The Bible, for all its amazingness, is just a book, after all, not God. In one example, the most earnest sola scriptura people increasingly focus on who to exclude, as if that equates with godliness. These churches and Christians invest a lot of energy in defining what is or isn't sin. Books are excellent if you want to draw lines against other people, which is why Jesus counted "lawyers" among his opponents—people whose specialty was parsing out the correct interpretation of words in books. Lawyers were all about who to exclude. Though unlike, say, Jesus, books do far worse at reaching out to *include* unexpected people.

My experience has been that it's not only the claim that the Bible is basically "clear" that's turned out to be false. It is also false that diligent Bible reading every day produces people who love and follow Jesus. Very few of my early Christian friends that I've kept up with are still daily Bible readers. For those, like me, who continued on: after a decade or two, pretty much everyone has needed to take a break and ask, what's really going on for them with all this reading? Are they now, God forbid, a little bored by the Bible? As a pastor of a large church for almost twenty years—who talks to lots and lots of other pastors—I can verify that advice to congregants to read the Bible every day is rarely taken. The Bible, again, is awesome, but it's not alive in the way that Jesus claims for himself.[21]

Sola scriptura turned out to be a great organizing principle for the modern world. Modernism is dominated by systems and machines. For committed modernists looking for a spiritual mechanism, what better than treating a *book* as the unchanging machine that will always spit out good results?

Jesus seemed to think that the Bible was very much meant to be the means to a different end than sola scriptura. There's, for instance, John 5:39: "You study the scriptures diligently because you think that in them you have eternal life. These are the very scriptures that testify about me." Maybe this focus on the Bible is, in the end, an old temptation, a way to feel in control of our lives and destinies which otherwise feel out of control. If we hated the vulnerability of being controlled by a capricious Pope and so put our stake in the ground that we weren't under the authority of the Pope, but of the Bible, then Jesus kicks that stick out from under us as well in Matthew 28

---

21 My sola scriptura friends might have a pointed rejoinder here. Not alive!? What about Hebrews 4:12? "For the word of God is alive and active. Sharper than any double-edged sword, it penetrates even to dividing soul and spirit, joints and marrow; it judges the thoughts and attitudes of the heart." Sounds like the scriptures are far from "dead words!" That might be a great point. However, the context of the verse has nothing to do with the Bible. It's talking about Jesus as the "word of God." Look at how this passage continues, "Therefore, since we have a great high priest who has ascended into heaven, Jesus the Son of God, let us hold firmly to the faith we profess … Let us then approach God's throne of grace with confidence, so that we may receive mercy and find grace to help us in our time of need." Throughout the letter to the Hebrews, the author again and again expresses great enthusiasm for knowing and following Jesus. It comes up chapter by chapter. The letter starts with a soliloquy about that. I'm not aware of similar enthusiasm in Hebrews for the Bible in a sola scriptura sense.

when he says, "All authority in heaven and on earth has been given to me." Not to the Bible but to the living, risen Christ. Jesus seems to think it's not all about the Bible. It's all about him.

He has a particularly useful and revealing take on this in Mark 4. You'll remember his parable of the sower and the soils. Listeners come from all over the area to hear from this amazing teacher and he tells an impenetrable story about how seeds only grow in a certain kind of soil. He warns his listeners that what he's saying is important. Most nonetheless leave immediately after he finishes. Then, his followers and a few others make their way to him to ask what on earth he was talking about. He tells them that they've been given "the secret of the kingdom of God" (which seems strange, since all they've said is that they have no idea what he was talking about) while, for those "outside" (seemingly everyone who didn't come find him to ask him what he was talking about) "everything is in parables" so that they might hear but not understand, and so wouldn't turn and be forgiven. For most readers, this is both baffling and troubling. Does Jesus not want everyone to "turn and be forgiven"? He intentionally tosses out an obscure teaching to make sure that lots of people *won't* go to heaven? We realize as he continues on that their "secret of the kingdom of God" is that they traipsed over to ask Jesus directly to explain his teaching. The secret of the kingdom of God turns out to be responding to the living, interactive Jesus. By contrast, at least some of his teaching— his words recorded in the Bible!—were intentionally impossible to understand. They were the opposite of "clear." His point seems to be that he wasn't interested in leaving behind a manual of his teachings for people to obey with or without him. He doesn't want people to believe they can "turn and be forgiven" because of their response to a book. He only offers himself to accomplish that.

If not sola scriptura, what's our counterproposal?[22] We're wondering if it's best framed by Phyllis Tickle in her book *The Great Emergence: How Christianity is Changing and Why*. She has a bold thought about how God works in history—namely that God changes the terms of following God every 500 years or thereabouts. Since Jesus' day (she says this pattern holds pre-Jesus as well), there's been Constantine, the schism between the Catholic and Orthodox churches, the Reformation, and then right now (which she calls "the Great Emergence"). The modern world effectively began with the Reformation, which made the mechanistic sola scriptura work well. But having moved into and beyond postmodernism, its flaws have shown themselves. The flaws, again, are not in the scriptures themselves, but in this modernistic take on them. What's needed in this new transition is Jesus. This, happily, is the appeal Jesus was making in the Bible itself.

So what does it mean to have "solus Jesus" as a primary framework? Sola scriptura had some practical advantages. It set itself up as a way to settle theological disputes, for instance. I hope it's not churlish to say that it was far less helpful in settling disputes than it promised because, again, its premise was off-base from the start. The scriptures were no more "clear" than Jesus' parable of the sower was, which led to a profession of theological lawyers much like the Pharisees had. The scriptures quite clearly supported slavery until they didn't and quite clearly supported Prohibition until they didn't and quite clearly insisted that women could never preach until they didn't. That is, until they didn't support such things. It turned out that the early Catholic critique of sola scriptura was borne out. But sola scriptura also suggested a straightforward means of growing in Jesus for a lifetime, which was to read the Bible

---

22 If you'd enjoy a book that delightfully messes with a sola scriptura "clear" reading of the Bible, and then proposes a new way to think about Bible reading, take a look at Peter Enns's *The Bible Tells Me So: Why Defending Scripture Has Made Us Unable to Read It* (HarperOne, 2015).

every day. Again, that program doesn't appear to do what it promised, but it was clear what you were supposed to do.

What are the implications of solus Jesus?

1. It relies on Jesus being alive and eager to speak to us.

This might understandably freak you out.

It feels so … subjective! (And we modernists hate subjectivity!) Just because you *say* you "heard from God" about this or that, why should I trust you? Why should you trust yourself?

And, indeed, that's a totally worthy line of conversation. But, whatever our concerns, Jesus seems fine with all that risk. There's that "secret of the kingdom of God" stuff. There's the Hebrews 10 encouragements to go to the throne of God because of Jesus. There's Matthew 11:28, "Come to me, all you who are weary and burdened, and I will give you rest."

So, for all the risks and the need for thoughtful pastoring and wise and loving community, are we advised to set up a system in which, for heaven's sake, we need to make sure *not* to require a living God?

2. Perhaps this loving, interactive Jesus is revealed to us in several important ways.

If the scriptures speak of Jesus (per John 5:39, quoted a few paragraphs back) and if the Holy Spirit also speaks of Jesus and if, together, people who follow Jesus get called "the body of Christ," then maybe we can help each other out in some key ways. Happily, the scriptures turn out to have a role to play! They just aren't the bottom line. But combined with hearing from Jesus by way of the Holy Spirit and with rich, transparent friendships with other people following Jesus, it sounds like we'll be on a good road.

3. It switches the focus from figuring out who to exclude, to believing God for new people to include.

Again, books are great for analyzing and line-drawing, but they're bad at doing surprising, loving things. They're not alive in that sense. But Jesus is not that way at all! Let's go back to our friend John, in 12:32, where Jesus says, "And I, when I am lifted up from the earth, will draw all people to myself." Far from figuring out who to exclude, Jesus has a specific, loving and expansive agenda. It was foreshadowed in the Hebrew Bible (in which Israel was called not to judge the surrounding nations, but to be a "light" to them). Then again in John, Jesus aggressively signals what he's about in some of his earliest words. This is 3:17: "For God did not send his Son into the world to condemn the world, but to save the world through him."

A switch in focus from exclusion to inclusion is a big deal.

4. **It suggests that the loving and interactive Jesus you meet will help you interpret the scriptures.**

Brother Lawrence (who is worth reading in so many ways that apply here) has a powerful word about this. He talks about how he speaks to God each night and confesses all his faults and sins. But, rather than getting God's rebuke, which he expects, what he gets is lavish love and regard. It seems scandalous! Shouldn't a serious Christian like Brother Lawrence be "serious about his sin?" Shouldn't he be "uncompromising?" Shouldn't he be "serious about personal holiness?" Well, on the one hand, *he* is *all* of those things! He's confessing his sins to God each night. The one who's *not* those things is *God*! Jesus, as experienced here, is so loving, encouraging and hope-filled that it changes Brother Lawrence's expectation of faith in such a way that people flock to him from throughout Europe. I've experienced what Brother Lawrence describes. Once that happens, when one reads the Bible, one understands it as coming from the heart of *that* loving God. My experience has been that the stern, line-drawing interpreters of "biblical Christianity" that I've run across do not, at first blush, talk about having met that God. In that respect, while of course making no comment at all about their internal love of God or their hopes for heaven, it doesn't seem obvious that we're worshipping the same God.

The Jesus I've met is not the stern judge they describe. Solus Jesus encourages reading the Bible with the lens of the Jesus you're getting to know.

Let's think now for a moment about how you and I might live out a solus Jesus faith. On the one hand, we'll need to figure this out together, if Ms. Tickle was right, because you and I are at the latest hinge of redemptive history in which this big change is just happening. I'm confident that whatever I say here will be only rudimentary thoughts, but let's start somewhere.

How can you be solus Jesus today?

1. Spend actual time with the living Jesus.

This is easier for some people than for other people. I'm not much of a Myers-Briggs personality profile person—I know only the most basic things about it—but I wonder if this is easier for what they'd call an "N" (an intuitive person) than it is for an "S" (a pragmatic, "sensate" person). One of my sons is very literal-minded and I've wondered if, for Jesus to "speak" to him, Jesus would have to show up in the flesh and be very explicit. This "talking with a God who talks back" concept is very intuitive. Revisiting my former playwright days, I've been listening to a radio theater version of George Bernard Shaw's *Saint Joan* recently. (The play is a stunner. The radio version by Hollywood Theatre of the Ear, with Amy Irving as Joan, is wonderful.) When Joan of Arc's opponents assert that what she calls the voice of God is in fact only her imagination, her response is, "Of course. How else can we hear God?" This is a particular skill, and an intuitive one. I like to walk and talk with Jesus. This helps me focus. But Grace gets distracted on walks and does better with a journal in which she writes her questions and tries to get a feel for what God might be saying back.

As hard to pin down as this practice is, it does seem to be near to Jesus' heart, as we learn in Mark 4 and in John 14:26.[23] If we're looking for Jesus himself to be our authority, it seems to follow that we'd be served by him speaking to us.

2. **Learn from everyone you can about this ongoing, chatty relationship with Jesus—and teach all the things you know.**

Thankfully, the "body of Christ" is one way Jesus tells us we'll get to experience him. Other people can help us in this, and we can help them as well. That body extends throughout history, so we can learn from Brother Lawrence, and Therese of Lisieux and many others. Discipleship will include an ever-expanding skill set.

3. **Enjoy the Bible in the company of this Jesus you're coming to know.**

In solus Jesus, you have nothing to fear from the Bible. Jesus is right there encouraging you as you read, and guiding you to fresh connection with him. This by no means excludes the kind of scripture "study" that I've given so many hundreds of hours to. The way scripture will take on the kind of life that Jesus promises in himself is if the living Jesus whom you're coming to know is right there with you as he shows you how the passages you're reading are all about him in some key ways.

4. **Embrace the mission of Jesus as your personal (and corporate) story.**

If Jesus came to seek and save those who are lost,[24] what would it look like to joyfully dream of that being your story as well, whatever your profession, whatever your life circumstances? What if this doesn't bring pressure or disapproval with it—for doing this well or poorly—but instead

---

23 "But the Advocate, the Holy Spirit, whom the Father will send in my name, will teach you all things and will remind you of everything I have said to you."

24 Luke 19:10

is an offer that the life of Jesus can be yours in some very real way in your actual circumstances?

5. Join others who are doing this.

Solus Jesus seems best to come to life when we find real partners and friends who are excited by pursuing this alongside us. Best case scenario: these people will be your friends in your church. But do this with others one way or another. It's just more fun and powerful that way.

What is our authority?

Is it a church leader?

Is it a book?

Let's band together and joyfully learn what the Bible so profoundly teaches—that Jesus, not a book or a fellow human being, is our Lord. He is our authority. He, being alive and loving, can be trusted with that task. And that's only good news, because for all the hardship of each of our lives, Jesus only brings good news.

3

Centered-Set Faith is the Absolute Best

I meet Muslims who follow Jesus.

AWHILE BACK I was in Beirut and a friend who lived there introduced me to some of his friends. They knew I was an American pastor and one of them introduced himself to me as a "Muslim who follows Jesus." This was a new category for me. "Oh!" I said. "So you're a Christian." The man took umbrage. "That's not what I said at all! I said I was Muslim!" I backpedaled. "I'm so sorry," I said. "I'm sure I just don't have the category for what you're talking about. It's just that in my world, when someone says they're following Jesus, by definition that makes them a 'Christian.'"

"Dave," he said, "I'm sure you're aware that Beirut, not long ago, went through a devastating civil war. In fact, I believe that, in the West, 'Beirut' became shorthand for 'a terrible war zone.' Do you remember who was fighting in that war?" "Well," I said tentatively, "I believe it was the Christians and the Muslims." "Exactly!" he said. "And I am a Muslim. The Christians were the ones killing my family members. Here is another question for you. Do you know how many Christians in Beirut go to church?" Obviously I didn't. "And I don't either!" he said. "Censuses are very sensitive things in Lebanon these days. But my guess would be under one percent." "Wow," I said. "Then what makes them 'Christians?'" "History!" he said. "Christians have been in Lebanon since not long after the time of the apostles. So there is a Christian *culture* that spans millennia. And there is a *Muslim* culture that spans almost as long.

My culture is *Muslim*. It does not mean that I'm especially religious—I grew up secular Muslim. But now I follow Jesus. So I am a Muslim who follows Jesus."

That raised all sorts of questions for me. Did he or his other "Muslim who follow Jesus" friends pray in the mosque? Were there any conflicts that came up between being Muslim and following Jesus?

But first I had an *aha* moment.

I turned to my friend who'd introduced us and said, "So, on those terms you'd be a 'Christian who follows Jesus.'" This was because my friend was the son of pastors. "Exactly!" my friend said. "Fascinating," I said. "And I by contrast would be a 'secular person who follows Jesus.'" "Yes!" my friend said.

Well. This explained a lot.

For instance, when I'd first started following Jesus, a few people had told me I needed to get rid of my secular music and listen to Christian music instead, that I should get rid of my secular books and read Christian books alone. This seemed crazy, especially because I was a music critic for a newspaper at the time and I was a college literature major.

The advice I got in that era came from Christians who saw their own culture as—obviously!—the good, godly one. What if it was, like my secular culture, just *their culture*? What if we *all* regard our culture as "the godly (or best) culture?" I knew that I felt a strong need to assert my culture as "better" than theirs—mine had Shakespeare and Miles Davis, while theirs had the *Left Behind* series and Michael W. Smith—which may or may not have been true, but the important insight was just that their culture wasn't my culture.

Maybe it comes down to your fourth-grade math class.

To get to the heart of what's been so helpful about my experience in Beirut, picture two sorts of sets.

The first is represented by a circle. We'll call this a bounded-set. The issue with a bounded-set is with people being inside of the circle or outside of it.

The second, though, has no "inside" or "outside." Picture a large dot in the center of a page that has lots of smaller dots on the page as well. The issue here is *motion*. Are the smaller dots moving towards the center dot or away from it?[25]

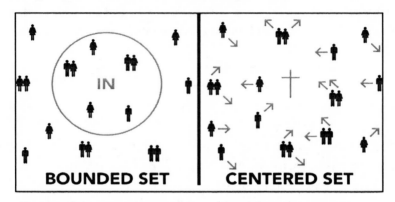

We all have bounded-sets, in terms of groups of people we feel comfortable with. "Muslim," to my new friend in Beirut, was his bounded-set, his culture, his people. Churches, in this view, are customarily bounded sets. In your or my church, we have our understanding of the "truth" inside of

25 The originator of this idea was a Fuller Theological Seminary anthropologist named Paul Hiebert. Many people have since written about bounded versus centered set, but Hiebert's original thoughts on the matter are hard to find. I believe he first wrote about this in "Conversion, Culture and Cognitive Categories" in Gospel in Context 1:4 (October, 1978), 24-29. (One reviewer writes this to me: "Hiebert's chapter "The Category Christian in the Mission Task" is contained in *Anthropological Reflections on Missiological Issues* [Baker Academic, 1994], which is still in print." If you'd like to track down his book.) All to say, Hiebert included another type of set that he called a "fuzzy set." I've gotten pushback that, to do justice to Hiebert, we need to think about all three of these sets working together. I've found that line of thought to be less helpful, so I'll leave that perspective for others to extol. The thoughts here are my own and those of Blue Ocean friends. We aren't attempting to represent Hiebert's thinking beyond our appreciation for the categories.

our boundaries with the hope that those outside will "cross the line" of our bounded set and join us in this good thing, maybe in this thing that will give them salvation. Perhaps we underestimate how much of our circle is cultural. And we underestimate how most of us, like my conversation partner in Beirut, aren't looking for other bounded sets to join.

Jesus does the heavy lifting.

So, the idea of centered-set faith[26] is that the center of the set is Jesus.[27] There is no "in" or "out," because there is no circle, but again, there is *motion* either towards the center or away from it. Jesus is no ordinary "center," because he's alive. When we turn towards Jesus, he's like the father in the parable of the Prodigal Son. The moment we turn towards him—wham!— he's running smack into us and calling for a great party. When we turn towards Jesus, *he* does the heavy lifting. When we turn away from him, there's no life to be found. Like the Prodigal Son, we're reduced to eating what the pigs eat.

In that sense, the stakes of centered-set faith in the first instance are *pragmatic* (are we finding actual life and

---

26 We've given some attention to what each distinctive is trying to accomplish. Though there are six of them, only one of them—"solus Jesus"—is our primary *framework*. Others involve things like our approach to spiritual development, or our approach to other churches. So, each distinctive is limited in what it's trying to address. This chapter looks at what we're calling our "primary metaphor." "Centered-set" is pervasive in our thinking. It's everywhere, including in all of the other distinctives, but it's a term from math. It's a way of looking at the world, a mindset. It's not set up to become, say, a rigorous theology. It is set up to suggest a mindset by which one might *arrive* at a rigorous theology.

27 I've led conversations about centered-set in varied settings. I talked about it in a group of inter-religious college chaplains who were looking to see if it would help them find more helpful, mutual conversations. I wondered with them if it could be helpful, one tier out from the center of their set, to think of something called, say, "the good life" or "what makes life worth living."

encouragement in Jesus? Are our lives getting better?) rather than *moral* (are we succeeding in keeping a list of religious rules? Do we hold the right religious opinions?). When bounded and centered-set believers get in a squabble, more often than not they miss each other because they're arguing based on two different standards. Stereotypically, the bounded-set believer will talk about sin; is x or y a sin and, if you don't think so, can you prove it? The centered-set believer will talk about fruit; does the outcome of a given doctrine lead to something good or something destructive?[28]

Just last weekend, a man paid some Blue Ocean friends a nice compliment. He'd heard them teach for a day and a half and he said not only was he interested throughout, but he noticed something. They were each light-hearted and, he felt, self-effacing in ways he wasn't used to hearing from people teaching him about religion. Was that just their temperaments, or was there some theological truism playing itself out there?

I think it boils down to centered-set. When you and I are in bounded-set, it seems to me, we spend most of our time looking at the boundaries. How do we know where the good zone-of-salvation ends and the bad zone-of-damnation begins? To answer this, we spend a good amount of time figuring out what is and isn't sin, because "sin" is what makes up the line of separation. It's a heavy responsibility! For pastors in bounded-set settings, we need to preach "the full counsel of God"[29] or we risk having other people's blood on our heads when they go to hell because we didn't tell them they'd crossed over the boundary into the land of sin. I get sent a lot of articles, or invited into a lot of Facebook conversations along these lines, and they're customarily pretty humorless and unhappy. Jesus tells us in Matthew 6 that "the eye is the

---

28 Per Matthew 7:16-18: "By their fruit you will recognize them. Do people pick grapes from thornbushes, or figs from thistles? Likewise, every good tree bears good fruit, but a bad tree bears bad fruit. A good tree cannot bear bad fruit, and a bad tree cannot bear good fruit."
29 Acts 20:27

lamp of the soul," as if what we look at will flood our souls, so we should choose our field of vision carefully. As the *GQ* writer a couple chapters back noticed about the megachurch pastor she was profiling, looking primarily at the *boundaries* of faith is to drink heavy, heavy responsibility into our spirits.

By contrast, in centered-set, we're looking as best as we can towards the center, who is the ever-delightful Jesus who loves us, speaks to us, encourages us and invites us to be flooded with his Holy Spirit at our very deepest levels. Here *Jesus* takes on all that burden and responsibility that, when we're looking towards the boundaries, we've taken on ourselves. I think what the man who complimented my friends was noticing was how mood-lightening it is to focus on Jesus as a primary activity.

How did Jesus mentor his followers?

Let's think for a moment about the stories in the gospels. Jesus calls people to follow him. They aren't asked to pass any orthodoxy tests (later on in the book of Acts, they discover that Jesus is directly leading them to clash with the orthodoxy of the time). Instead, they learn by following him—literally, walking along beside him and being with him. Every now and again—Matthew 10 and the sending of the 72 for instance— he gives them object lessons to help them experience what following him as a living God and guide will be like once he's gone. Keep this picture in mind as we keep talking.

I visit churches and get a surprise.

I have an interesting case study. After almost two decades of (unexpectedly) pastoring a church, my family and I have now had several years of attending churches we're not leading. We've met nice people and enjoyed dynamic worship and been impressed by things these churches do well. (Kudos to the greeter who met us in the parking lot and personally escorted us to all of our kid's classes!) We've had some surprises, maybe the most striking of which came with a sudden realization after one Sunday service at a church we'd gone to many times.

"You know," I said to a friend who was a longtime attendee at this evangelical church, "there are definitely things to recommend this church. But you know one subject I don't believe we've heard discussed in all the sermons we've heard? Jesus! That seems like a surprising omission." Our friend nodded. "Yup," he said. "Jesus pretty much never comes up."

It struck me how long it had taken me to notice this. How had I missed it? I think it was because seemingly *related* subjects had come up, like "a biblical worldview."[30] Certainly passages from the Bible were discussed each time. But Jesus as a subject of interest? Never.

That got Grace and me thinking about all of the churches we'd visited, half a dozen or so. Had Jesus come up in *those* services? After pondering that, it seemed that he hadn't.

Now, we said to one another, surely the pastors in question *thought* they'd talked about Jesus, in their way. We didn't doubt any of their sincerity, but I think they were steeped in the responsibilities of bounded-set.

Centered-set hits a major snag, which is solved with a big brainstorm.

In a moment, I'll try to flesh out how living out one's day in centered-set looks different than living it out in bounded-set. I'll look at some of the many objections that come to mind for my friends who are steeped in bounded-set faith, but first let's look at one potentially major deal-breaker.

My friend Dan loves centered-set. He would tell you it's been central in his being able to follow Jesus at all. However,

---

30 I've come to believe that "a biblical worldview" is a catchphrase for "figuring out what is and isn't sin." When we have more time, there's a lot to talk about *modernism*—the way of looking at the world that came to us in the Enlightenment and that was originally the great enemy to people of faith before being embraced by most of them. Our current incarnation of bounded-set—as seen in phrases like "a biblical worldview"—is profoundly modernist.

as someone whose friends are by and large non- churchgoers, he pointed out a consequential problem.

Namely, while it helped him follow Jesus in a way that nothing else had, it turned out to be unhelpfully binary in his relationships. Let's say he was talking with an atheist friend. Either he'd help his friend turn his arrow towards Jesus or, God forbid, his friend would turn Dan's arrow *away from* Jesus. The stakes were high!

But what, Dan suggested, if we all have more than one arrow? What if people are more complicated than that? What if we all have, say, a hundred arrows?

Let's say, in this imagined conversation with his atheist friend, his conversation about Jesus went nowhere. Then, what if his friend made an impassioned appeal to Dan to be much more environmentally aware than Dan was—to recycle, compost, watch his water usage and install solar panels, to think about the impact of his environmental choices on the rest of the planet? What if Dan, rattled by this, asked Jesus about it later in the day? What if Jesus responded, "Oh, your friend is totally right. Change your ways." In this scenario, who turned whose arrow towards Jesus? The answer: Dan's atheist friend turned one of *Dan's* arrows towards the center. It's worth noting in this example that the center *isn't* "being environmentally conscious" or "caring for the earth." It's still *Jesus*. After all, Jesus himself validated Dan's friend's appeal. Dan's atheist friend, in this instance, knew something about Jesus that Dan needed to know.

Suddenly all of our relationships come alive. What does that person right in front of us—whatever their religion or lack thereof—know about Jesus that we need to know?

This messes with "evangelism."
(Thank God! Evangelism is the worst.)

My church in Cambridge, Massachusetts saw hundreds and hundreds of people experience faith in Jesus during my time there. One regional nonprofit that helped evangelical churches become better at evangelism said that we were 1400 percent more effective evangelistically than the most successful churches they worked with.

Yet, I can't imagine an attendee in our church that wouldn't viscerally reject the thought of evangelism.

Maybe a quick story will illustrate this. One woman who found faith with us, who'd never attended a church before ours, said she'd be out the door immediately if we ever told her to "evangelize her friends." Evangelism was offensive to her, as if she'd suddenly become "right" about something and all her friends and family members were "wrong." As if she wasn't just one person in a sea of other smart, thoughtful people. As if she was saying she was better than them.

The next Sunday she introduced me to six of her friends that she'd brought to church.

She told me they each loved it! It was fantastic!

I pulled her aside. Just to check in—hadn't she, only days before, told me with quite a bit of passion that she'd rather die than evangelize anyone? So what was all this?

Suddenly her passion returned. This wasn't *evangelism*! *Ick*! As *if*! She just thought that our church was great, that I was great, that I talked about helpful things about Jesus that her friends would really appreciate, and so she invited them and discovered she was right! So, was it was *okay* with me that she'd invited her friends, or was I saying that our church was only for Christians and not for other nice people who'd like to learn how to follow Jesus?!

Here's another intriguing case study, this one from the recent Blue Ocean conference I mentioned. For unrelated reasons, a secular Muslim Pakistani woman asked if she could drop by the conference to meet me. She sat through the first *two hours* of the teaching there—quite a download of thoughts, even for the most devoted churchgoer, including quite a few thoughts on centered-set faith. "That was amazing!" she said when she introduced herself. "I've never been in a church before, but I love it! Because what you all are saying is that

Jesus is for everyone, not just for Christians! I've never heard such a thing!" Later that afternoon, she went to a workshop led by a fellow Blue Ocean pastor about a method to invite Jesus into our circumstances that's called Immanuel Prayer. My new friend found me afterwards. "Oh my gosh!" she said. "That was tremendously powerful! I was planning to meet you and then leave, but now I'd like to come back to the rest of the conference if you'll let me."

How is it that, in my experience, the most effective "evangelistic" strategy is utterly to avoid evangelism? I think it's that, when we point people towards Jesus, Jesus himself does the work of proving himself loving and powerful. One of my friends makes the distinction this way: We're invited to be "witnesses" to Jesus, but we're prohibited from being "advocates" for him. We're prohibited from arguing his case. That role is reserved for the Holy Spirit.

What does centered-set faith look like in one's actual day?

In the last chapter, I detailed some implications of living out solus Jesus as opposed to living out sola scriptura. Those implications apply here—for our purposes, solus Jesus relates to centered-set faith and sola scriptura relates to bounded-set faith. You'll note that they all circle the idea of focusing on the living, communicating Jesus and letting him guide and encourage you.

- Spend actual time with the living Jesus.
- Learn from everyone you can about this ongoing, chatty relationship with Jesus, and teach all the things you know.
- Enjoy the Bible in the company of this Jesus you're coming to know.
- Embrace the mission of Jesus as your personal (and corporate) story.
- Join others who are doing this.

So that's the very simple spirit of it. Centered-set faith
means you try to listen to and follow Jesus and look for the
good things that will happen as you do. It's to believe that, like
the good shepherd he claims to be, Jesus is always looking
to guide and encourage you, and lead you into great pasture.
Always, and at every moment, as he did with his apostles
during his earthly ministry. As a pastor, you're trying to help
your congregants experience each passage you preach on in
that light. How does the passage help you experience the living
Jesus better? It's simple, but it can take quite a bit of focus and
reflection to stay on track.

You're pushing this too far!

I know dozens of pastors in a denomination that's talked
about centered-set for years. Initially, they love conversations
like the one we're having here. But then—given that the
denomination is firmly evangelical—they do need to push
back. Yes, they'll say, centered-set is great and really important.
I'm centered-set myself—they'll say—absolutely! We could
never go to that legalistic, bounded-set church down the
street! But, I mean, let's be serious. If you read the Bible even
a little bit (and, Dave, you do read the Bible at least a *little*
bit, don't you?) clearly it's loaded to the gills with boundaries.
Even if we could agree that normal congregants could in some
sense be centered-set, surely *leaders* in our churches need to
embrace the boundaries. So, a mature approach to centered-
set is to realize that it means *bounded*-set, but, well, *nicer*.

But it seems to me that, no, they're actually different sets
that operate on different rules. And Jesus and Paul and Peter
and the rest of the New Testament are insistent upon centered-
set.[31] So, I'm centered-set all the way.

---

31 One picture: Paul in Galatians 5:11: "If I am still preaching
circumcision (his stand-in for "following the rules of the Bible" or
"bounded-set"), why am I still being persecuted?" His point? Religious
people love you when you tell them that their bounded set is the

To someone steeped in bounded-set, this might seem crazy. How could this be possible? It would upset every assumption about … everything!

Let me list some objections that come up from my bounded-set friends and offer brief thoughts in response.

1. **In the end, even centered-set is bounded. The "line" in question here is just defined as "separating those moving towards Jesus from those moving away from him." Voila: Two sets. Bounded-set!**

    I find myself impatient with this one, as I find it comes from a hope of landing a "gotcha" moment without a need to engage at all. Centered-set is not, in fact, bounded-set. Centered-set is a different sort of set that has no in or out, only motion. To see this as bounded is to refuse to consider that other sorts of sets are possible. They're different mindsets.

    That said, one friend of mine, who is by no means hostile to centered-set, does push back that centered-set is still a *set*, which means that by nature it sets up parameters to figure out who's in the set (of people who live their lives according to centered-set) and who isn't, so perhaps there is a distant "boundary" worth noting. However, in my view, all of the usefulness here comes from taking centered-set on its own terms.

2. **Centered-set isn't rigorous like bounded-set is. Anything goes when there are no boundaries!**

    Let's play "on the one hand, on the other hand."

    On the one hand, touché! In a centered-set world, you do lose a laser-focus on rules, directing your focus instead towards Jesus. Rules, as Paul tells us, motivate us to do right and avoid wrong out of fear. Obey, or else! There are big consequences—salvation or damnation—riding on our obedience or disobedience to the rules.

    Most definitely, in a bounded-set world, not much goes.

---

one God likes, but the second you preach only Jesus (in other words, become centered-set), the knives come out.

In centered-set, we're motivated by outcomes, by what Jesus calls "fruit." And, in my experience, this brings a sort of real-world rigor that bounded-set doesn't have.

In bounded-set, the issue is getting inside of the boundary, after which the stakes mostly boil down to staying within the boundaries and hoping your kids don't drift outside. In centered-set, you're following the living Jesus, who will actually take you somewhere if you hope to stay close to him. Jesus, for instance, recently seemed to direct my wife and me to leave behind our prestigious jobs (and secure salaries) and move our family thousands of miles away while trusting him for money. All in service of new ways we could engage with his mission. After a lengthy time of prayer and having others pray for us and getting other people's perspective on this crazy idea, we did it. In my circles, this sort of thing isn't exceptional. My centered-set friends commonly take consequential risks of faith.

Let's take a moment again to consider the idea of "sin." The word means "missing the mark"—which, you've got to say, sounds pretty centered-set. When our arrows "miss the mark" of pointing towards Jesus, we get reality-based feedback; we don't get the kind of life, hope and comfort in our problems and sense of meaning, connection and joy that Jesus gives us when we follow him.[32] At those times, we're encouraged to "repent," of which a primary definition is to "turn again" or "recalibrate"—to turn your arrow back towards Jesus who loves

---

32 A noteworthy verse along these lines is John 10:27-28, in which Jesus says, "My sheep listen to my voice; I know them, and they follow me. I give them eternal life, and they shall never perish; no one will snatch them out of my hand." Evidently what it means to be "Jesus' sheep" is that we (A) listen to his actual voice and (B) follow where he goes. As we do this, he knows us—because we're in living relationship with him—and he leads us in actual fact (as opposed to "leading us" in some sort of abstract way based on religious commitments we've made) right into heaven, protecting us from threats every step of the way. Pretty encouraging stuff!

you, and away from the false gods that have no life in them, that lead only to misery. This is a profoundly rigorous—and wonderful!—project.

For instance, as you look at your heart right now, are you encouraged in your life with Jesus, or are the stresses of life pulling you into anxiety or unhappiness?[33]

3. Let's face it. The Bible is full of rules—yes, in the Old Testament, but no less so in the New Testament.

I quoted Paul in a footnote as being Mr. Centered-Set, but Paul also wrote Titus 1:6-8. "An elder must be blameless, faithful to his wife, a man whose children believe and are not open to the charge of being wild and disobedient. Since an overseer manages God's household, he must be blameless—not overbearing, not quick-tempered, not given to drunkenness, not violent, not pursuing dishonest gain. Rather, he must be hospitable, one who loves what is good, who is self-controlled, upright, holy and disciplined. He must hold firmly to the trustworthy message as it has been taught, so that he can encourage others by sound doctrine and refute those who oppose it." Isn't this directly saying that, if you want to "disciple" someone into leadership, you'll need to teach them to do the things Paul lists here, to follow the rules?

Well, let me offer a thought experiment.

Let's say you train someone to do all of this stuff and to hold the right creed, but that person doesn't know and follow the *living* Jesus. Except for that, though, they're perfect along these lines. Are you happy with how your coaching of them is going?

I think what we have here is a question of the cart and the horse. In bounded-set settings, we major on things like this list of behaviors as evidence of being "serious about God." I'd start in another place: with knowing and experiencing the living Jesus, to "knowing nothing except Christ and him

---

33 As per Mark 4:7—"Other seed fell among thorns, which grew up and choked the plants, so that they did not bear grain."

crucified"[34] as a first impulse. Paul's lists here would certainly make for great conversation fodder with someone who fully lives this out. The lists don't do as well without that. Taken as strict rules, this list requires parsing in the way the religious "lawyers" parsed the Torah in Jesus' day. For instance, a number of our most famous conservative Christian leaders have had children who quite publicly rebelled against the faith of their parents and become "wild and disobedient." Franklin Graham—now as fundamentalist a Christian as we have in the public sphere—famously left faith for many years on just these terms. I don't remember Billy Graham stepping down from Christian leadership at that time, and I'm glad he didn't! Still, that tells me that everyone, even the most-conservative Christians, understands that there's more to the faith Paul describes than strict rules can allow for. We're misreading him if we don't understand that he's inviting us into a much bigger world.

4. **The greatest thinkers about God are bounded-set, because thinking requires making distinctions—drawing boundaries!**

Well, given that I regard Jesus, Peter, Paul and David as centered-set, I'm not willing to write them off as second-rate theologians. But this does take me back to when I first started following Jesus.

Again, I grew up secular. What provoked my change of heart wasn't any smart argument by a religious person, it was an encounter with Jesus. I learned later on about this school of thought called "Christian apologetics," in which arguments for the rationality of believing in Jesus are suggested. It was nothing but fun to learn those arguments, to learn about Chuck Colson's or Josh McDowell's arguments for the truth of the resurrection. Or to read the favorite apologist of all of my new friends, C.S. Lewis, and learn that Jesus evidently had to either be (1) lying, (2) crazy or (3) God—and he didn't seem like a liar or an insane person so logically he had to be

---

34 1 Corinthians 2:2

God. This was juicy stuff![35] For old-school apologetics fans, there was Pascal's Wager (if you choose to believe in God, you risk nothing and have the possibility of gaining everything (heaven); if you disbelieve in God, you risk everything (hell) and gain nothing). I just loved this stuff. I read all of Lewis' works multiple times. G.K. Chesterton became a lasting favorite.

Then, I ended up helping to start this church in which many hundreds of people experienced Jesus from the non-churchgoing world. A far as I know, not one started following Jesus because of a conversation around apologetics. Not one.[36] I've come to believe that apologetics are wonderful for Christians (at least those who, like me, enjoy such things) because they'll give them confidence in the intellectual validity of their faith. That's a fun thing, but the claim of apologetics—that, to see the error of their ways, non-churchgoers only need what Peter called "the reason for the hope you have"[37]—has not been borne out in my experience. Centered-set, by contrast, is good news to the entire world.

---

35 If, sadly, since debunked in many settings I've been in where it's been hazarded.

36 As I was promoting my book *Not the Religious Type* some years back, I did several radio shows that focused on apologetics—I think the bookers had the mistaken belief that my book *was* apologetics because it talked about lots of people experiencing faith. When they found out that we were talking about different things, sometimes they were indignant. I explored this with one host. "So you host a regular show on Christian apologetics. You must be excited to see people experience faith in Jesus." "Absolutely!" he said. "My whole ministry is about convincing the secular world to come to Jesus." "And," I asked, "how many people have you seen experience Jesus as a result of your apologetics?" "Well," he said, "none. But that's because they're deceived and won't admit the superiority of my arguments."

37 1 Peter 3:15. Maybe a better way to look at the "reason" Peter is talking about here is not to regard it as apologetics-style abstractions, but as the actual way Jesus has changed your life.

There are many more objections we could chat about. If my Facebook page is to be believed, the way for Christians to be relevant to our changing cultures is to offer opinions on current cultural issues. This can be either from a conservative perspective (which regards most current cultural issues as evidence of a cultural rot that needs vigorously to be fought) or from a progressive one (which demonstrates to secular friends that conservative Christians aren't the only voices speaking for faith). Both of those are bounded sets (one of which I'm in, and so, since those posts are the voice of my people, I cheer them on). But can centered-set take on this prophetic role? Great question! Yes, it can! In fact to my mind it's the only hope of Jesus-based connection within the larger culture.

Let's close by looking at a few final implications of how centered-set plays out as we pursue it.

1. Centered-set creates a non-anxious system.

At the center of this system is Jesus who knows you, loves you and has done all the work to make the way to him and his father possible. So, if we move towards him, it can only be good news because there's no possibility that he'll reject us! As with the parable of the Prodigal Son and the experience of people like Brother Lawrence, it's settled that we'll get a warm reception. The risk in bounded-set is that it feeds on fear and insecurity. Our inside-ness can always be in doubt; we can legitimately and needfully get baptized again and again, and other people may well weigh in on our standing with God.

2. It reintroduces "I don't know" as a central theological statement.

I rarely do a gathering where someone doesn't point out how often I or the other presenters say "I don't know." After a recent conference, a church small group did a session on the theological significance of "I don't know."

Now, on the one hand, I and my fellow presenters do know some stuff! I do have a graduate degree in theology. I've read the Bible dozens and dozens of times. I'm familiar with the theological concepts that are important to my bounded-set friends. I've preached my thousand sermons, all of which included large swaths of scripture.

Then, what's with the incessant "I don't knows?"

In centered-set, no one can master *Jesus*. Where is he leading you or me in a given moment? Even on moral questions, which in bounded-set are the most important things to be "clear" about, a good deal of helpful "I don't know" creeps in.[38] What this assumes is that the living Jesus does have answers to our pressing questions, that he's very much accessible as we look to him and that the way we can best help our friends in their problems starts with humility, prayer and good listening.

You're picking up that centered-set, in looking to get the benefits of a living relationship with a living Jesus rather than settling for being good rules-keepers who stay comfortably within our bounded-set, is willing to embrace some degree

---

38 I have an anecdote on this that is perhaps too tidy, but it's fun! A prominent church that was looking to be centered-set that I connected with a few years back had unexpected success seeing, of all populations, international arms dealers come to Jesus. One pastor talked about mentoring one of these men. One day, the man asked his mentor, "Should I quit smoking?" The mentor, centered-set all the way, said, "Well, what's Jesus telling you?" The man took a moment to ask Jesus and then reported back, "He's telling me I should finish smoking the pack I'm on, really enjoy each smoke, and then never smoke again." And that's what the man did. A little later, the man asked the mentor, "Should I continue to have sex with my girlfriend or should I stop until we get married?" The church was a conservative church with explicit guidelines on such things, but the pastor stuck to his guns. "What's Jesus saying to you?" The man asked Jesus and then reported back, "Well, at the very least he's saying I should ask her to marry me!" And that's what he did.

of mess that few bounded-set people could happily take on. If the task of a Christian leader is primarily to make sure that our flock doesn't wander beyond the boundaries, we require "clarity." As we've talked about, the scriptures have to be "clear" on all things or our system falls apart. In centered-set, a good deal of "beats me" is married to a living, hopeful connection to the Jesus who promises to lead us to good pasture if we follow where he takes us.

3. It offers a newfound encouragement to cheer up.

My experience in bounded-set is that we're encouraged to be "sober-minded."[39] Yes, of course there's a longstanding Christian tradition of "the joy of the Lord" and of the need to "praise God." But, as we've discussed, in bounded-set what's more important is that we're playing for serious stakes! But if we're doing a profoundly different thing and looking at the living Jesus, he seems to be much more light-hearted than we are. Yes, the stakes of our lives are always intense—there are always circumstantial threats that are very real in every human life. There are genuinely sad things in our lives, and we'll be served by growing into the full range of our emotions. There are overwhelming societal problems. But this is not the same as "maturely" being *burdened*. Jesus' encouragement is to come to *him* when we're heavy laden, because *he* can bear those burdens while we can't. If there's a particular sin to consider in centered-set, refusing to take our burdens to Jesus would be a prime one![40] In my experience, we need permission to cheer up, a permission which rarely comes. Centered-set gives that permission.

---

39 1 Peter 5:8

40 Matthew 11:28-29: "Come to me, all you who are weary and burdened, and I will give you rest. Take my yoke upon you and learn from me, for I am gentle and humble in heart, and you will find rest for your souls." And, while I've got you, here's 1 Peter 5:7: "Cast all your anxiety on him because he cares for you."

4. It encourages us to embrace our vulnerability.

Jesus famously says "I am the way, the truth and the life."[41] In bounded-set, this is the central exclusionary verse. It seems worth noting that Jesus doesn't say that his *teaching* is all of that. Instead, *he* is all of that. Clearly this is not to disregard what he taught, but to recognize that, like the apostles, we're encouraged to find our way, truth and life with him as the good shepherd. This—as my family has discovered again in our recent move—makes one vulnerable. Here's Dietrich Bonhoeffer: "The disciple is dragged out of [our] relative security into a life of absolute insecurity (that is, in truth, into the absolute security and safety of the fellowship of Jesus) ... And if we answer the call of discipleship, where will it lead us?... To answer this question we shall have to go to him, for only he knows the answer. Only Jesus Christ, who bids us follow him, knows the journey's end. But we do know that it will be a road of boundless mercy. Discipleship means joy."[42]

Centered-set faith is the absolute greatest.

---

41 John 14:6.

42 Dietrich Bonhoeffer, *The Cost of Discipleship* (Macmillan, 1963), pp. 62-63, 41.

4

Childlike Faith Turns Out to Be the Only Road to Our Growth in God

"Where's the Adult Education Department?"

SHE WAS NICE, but no doubt had an edge.

"So," she said, "there's lots of really great stuff in your church. Lots of enthusiastic young people, a lot of people experiencing faith in Jesus for the first time, a lot of diversity, a lot of care for poor people in the city, lots of prayer and faith, a lot of risk-taking for God. Three cheers for you all! But—" (And hadn't I seen the "but" coming?) "—where's the adult education department?"

I asked her what she meant.

"The adult education department. The way that experienced Christians grow in Christian faith." I was still at a loss, so I asked her to fill that out. She said, "Like you, for instance, went to a theological seminary, right?" I said that I had but, with a few exceptions, it hadn't done a lot for my growth in faith. It was great for a lot of things! But not that. "Hmmm," she said, squinting a bit more. This wasn't looking good. "So you don't think you could offer some of that seminary stuff here? Stuff like a systematic theology class?" It was likely just my quirk, but I'd disliked systematic theology, had found it actively damaging to someone trying to follow Jesus. I thought for a moment, and told her that those hadn't been my favorite classes. "Hmmm," she said again, "Church history?" Certainly helpful in the big picture and I'd love to chat with her about whatever interested her along these lines, but we still seemed to be missing each other. "Ah-huh. Even Reformation history? It's always good to talk about the Reformers." I thought I might now be able to cut to the chase.

"So," I hazarded, "it seems like your feeling is that adults grow in faith the best when they learn graduate-level academic stuff about theology or church history. Is that what you're driving at?" It was, she said. Absolutely.

I have not found that to be true. I find it hard to imagine that was the plan Jesus had in mind. Now, on the one hand, most of my friends tend to be more, rather than less invested in theology and intellectual pursuits, but I'm not sure that equates to what she was calling "growth." I have seen hundreds of people experience what, to the eye of an outside observer, looked like tremendous growth in faith in Jesus. From the inside, it feels like *I've* grown in faith in Jesus.

How do Christians grow in faith?

Do we best grow in faith by learning new and interesting things? Or do we grown by some sort of journey of faith?

Or maybe it doesn't matter if we grow at all.

Let's stick with this last point for a minute.

Let's take faith from a bounded-set perspective for a moment. In bounded-set, the key issue is that you're inside the boundary. You've done everything you need to know that you're going to heaven! So … what's next? Well, of first importance is making sure that you stay inside, that you don't drift back into the realm of the damned. In that spirit, keeping a close eye on what is and isn't sin and making sure that you're not sinning (or that, if you are, you're quickly confessing) is a big deal. It's also helpful to have the "right" opinions on moral issues when it comes to who *else* is sinning! We get encouraged to "take stands" on the right moral issues and be on God's side in the controversy of the day on our Facebook page.

Now, there's some disagreement even about these things. A popular theology of a few decades back was shorthanded into the phrase "once saved, always saved." It—an extremely bounded-set perspective—argued that, if you've done all the needed things to be saved (told Jesus that you believed in him and asked for your sins to be forgiven, in the most rudimentary understanding), you unshakably could know that, whatever you might do or not do from this day forward, you were going to heaven.

On those terms, what was left to be done between now and the next life? Well, there were an enormous amount of things you might be *encouraged* to do! Those things might involve evangelism, or caring for poor people. Maybe your church strongly felt that you needed to advocate for a particular political perspective.

However, in the end, if you're in, you're in.

So—in this view—maybe "personal spiritual growth" is not the bottom line. It's a nice add-on, to be sure. How many of us, after all, like to stagnate? The biggest thing—your salvation— is taken care of whether you grow or not. That might explain why a common complaint in bounded-set faith settings is that people are bored. They've heard it all! Surely there's more to life than hearing another endless stream of sermons! My "adult education" conversation was along these lines— that maybe a key way to alleviate the boredom of "mature Christians" who've heard it all is to tell them at least a few things that they *haven't* heard before! Even if those things are pretty abstract.

As someone who's learned many of those "advanced" things, for all their delights I can say that they quickly run dry, leaving us in the same, aimless place that we were before.

Jesus proposes an answer.

Jesus directs us another direction entirely in Matthew 18 and 19 (as well as in Mark 10 and Luke 9 and 18) when he encourages us to pursue faith as if we were small children. He says this a lot and in multiple ways—like this, for instance: "Truly I tell you, unless you change and become like little children, you will never enter the kingdom of heaven."[43] He does seem to have a bee in his bonnet about mistakenly thinking that growth in faith boils down to getting more knowledge.[44]

On the one hand, this seems scandalous! Aren't we talking about how to *grow* in faith—where the point, presumably, is to become *mature* in our experience of God? In 1 Corinthians 13:11, doesn't Paul encourage us to "put the ways of childhood *behind* (us)?" Doesn't Hebrews 5 chew out its readers for being milk-drinking *babies* rather than meat-eating *grownups*?

But Jesus is calling us back to something more fundamental—to the very beginning of the Bible, to the story of the fall of humankind in which Adam and Eve are commanded by God not to eat the fruit of the tree of the knowledge of good and evil. In bounded-set, this is pretty straightforward: do the things God tells you to do! Don't sin! Stay within the boundaries! Still, it's fascinating to look at the story itself a little more closely, as Jesus encourages us to do. This forbidden tree, for instance, *didn't* give them their first introduction to right and wrong. We can presume that God would want them to have that introduction, and not keep them from it. Instead, this was a temptation towards discovering how to run their lives towards a happy future *without God*, to "be like God" to themselves, to take control of

---

43 Matthew 18:13

44 In Matthew 11:25-26, for instance. "At that time Jesus said, 'I praise you, Father, Lord of heaven and earth, because you have hidden these things from the wise and learned, and revealed them to little children. Yes, Father, for this is what you were pleased to do.'"

"good" and "evil" *outcomes* to their life choices. Where, before they ate this fruit, they perfectly trusted this all-good, all-knowing God to give them a great life, by doing this they were declaring that they were eager to go at it alone.

In that spirit, here's a useful quote I learned from my seminary education, from Martin Luther.

> *"Could we ascribe to a man anything greater than truthfulness and righteousness and perfect goodness? On the other hand, there is no way in which we can show greater contempt for a man than to regard him as false and wicked and to be suspicious of him, as we do when we do not trust him."*[45]

At the moment they ate the fruit, Adam and Eve were offering Luther's greatest of all insults to God—formally declaring that, despite all evidence to the contrary, they didn't trust that God's whole passion in life was to do them good with all his heart and soul.[46]

When they eat the fruit, when they fly their flag that they don't trust God to look out for them and take their lives to a good place, their immediate response is *shame*. They recognize immediately that they've bitten off a whole lot more than they can chew. They can't possibly figure out how to navigate themselves into a great, happy life—it's too big a task for any human being. Here's a related thought experiment.

---

45 "The Freedom of a Christian," in *Martin Luther: Selections from His Writings*, John Dillenberger [Doubleday, 1961], p. 59.

46 I'm quoting Jeremiah 32:40-41 here. One professor of mine called it "the plaque on God's wall." "I will make an everlasting covenant with them: I will never stop doing good to them … I will rejoice in doing them good … with all my heart and soul." (The professor, by the way, was Daniel P. Fuller, who shaped many of the points in this section. His big book on the subject—not the easiest read, but a seminal book for me—was *The Unity of the Bible: Unfolding God's Plan for Humanity* [Zondervan, 2000].)

Imagine that you're a three-year-old child in downtown Manhattan who says to your parent, "Hey, thanks so much for all your help to this point. I totally appreciate it! But, you know, I'm good at this point and I don't think I'll need you anymore. I can take things from here. I'll get a job, get a lease on a nice apartment, and set myself up just great. But thanks again for everything!"

Back to Jesus. In Matthew 18:13, he gives us the antidote to the fall of humankind—"Change and become like little children." When we "become like little children," we recognize that we *are*, in *fact*, that child of three in the middle of Manhattan. This time, though, we also recognize that our loving parent is right beside us, that they haven't gone anywhere despite what we said, that we had a moment of (thankfully) temporary insanity. "Becoming like little children" means that we take all our cares to God as if he actually cares and will help. Jesus directly tells us this a few chapters earlier in Matthew: "Come to me, all you who are weary and burdened, and *I* will give you rest."[47] "Cast all your anxiety on him," Peter tells us later on in the New Testament, "because he cares for you."[48] It requires a supernaturally powerful God and encourages ever-growing faith and prayer along those lines.

So then, how do we grow in faith? We take Jesus' antidote to the fall. Growth entirely boils down to childlike faith. It's the only plan there is, or has ever been. It's the whole ballgame.

Let's think about a few implications of childlike faith being our only hope of growth.

1. God is only good and does only good things for us.

My life—maybe like your life—often feels overwhelming. Years ago, I remember a one-panel comic taped to the front of an often-frazzled friend's refrigerator: it showed a woman having coffee and regretfully saying, "My life would be so much better if it were being lived by someone else."

47 Matthew 11:28
48 1 Peter 5:7

I know some people who pick a Bible verse as their "life verse." I think that comic must be my life comic.

Just yesterday, I took a pass at solving an organizational problem and almost immediately wondered if I'd messed up. What did God think about my choice? Even if God seemed to be on my side, was I still going to be happy with what came *out* of the choice? In retrospect, what if I'd tried to achieve the same goal in a different *way*? Now that I thought about it, *obviously* I should have taken a different tack! Oh *no*! What were the consequences of choosing Tack A rather than Tack B?!

And then God seemed to break in with completely different advice.

"Or," he seemed to say, "you could take the advice of King David in the Psalms and praise me for exactly how things are, whether you made the perfect choice or a poor choice. You could praise me for what actually *is*, in trust that I'm *great* at working with what actually is! You could give me all those consequences you're afraid of and you could trust me to do right by you and by all the other people involved." And so, that's what I did and—after an hour of having berated myself—I felt great.

Here's a question: What if, say, we are that child of three in the big city? What if, as argued here, our parent hasn't gone anywhere despite our telling him or her that we want to take things alone from here on out? Then, a cloud crosses our once-sunny perspective on the situation—what if this parent on occasion has their own agenda that might not match up all that well with our agenda for our own life? I mean, that wouldn't feel so great.

As a place to start on that question, check out Psalm 147:10-11,

> *His pleasure is not in the strength of the horse, nor his delight in the power of human legs; the LORD delights in those who fear him, who put their hope in his unfailing love.*

Evidently, God doesn't cheer up when he sees how strong and awesome we are at solving our own problems. He cheers up when we "put our hope in *his* unfailing love!" He's happy when we believe that he's actually good, that he actually loves us and that we can actually trust him in actual things! Jonathan Edwards put it this way: God's holiness consists in his delight in himself. God knows that he's completely good and trustworthy towards us—for him to be holy means that he *can't back down* on that point. If he indicated in any way that we might be better off looking elsewhere for a happy life, he'd be *lying* to us, and thereby unholy. He tells us in Exodus 33:18-19[49] that his "glory" is exactly the same as his being good towards us. He gets glory when we're satisfied customers who go to him with all of our problems.[50]

In an earlier footnote, I called Jeremiah 32:40-41 "the plaque on God's wall:"

"I will make an everlasting covenant with them: *I will never stop doing good to them* … I will rejoice in doing them good … with all my heart and soul."

What's on God's agenda today? Doing good things for you! And then, after lunch, doing a few *more* good things for you! That's what makes him happy—he "rejoices" to do you good![51]

Jeremiah 29:11 famously tells us that God's been putting some real thought into what his plan for the rest of your life is,

---

49 Then Moses said, "Now show me your glory." And the LORD said, "I will cause all my goodness to pass in front of you."

50 Psalm 116 is amazing on this point. "What shall I return to the Lord/ for all his goodness to me? I will lift up the cup of salvation/ and call on the name of the Lord." How can I pay God back for bailing me out when I really need it? The next time I'm in trouble, I promise to go to him to bail me out again!

51 James 1:17 works this point. "Every good and perfect gift is from above, coming down from the Father of the heavenly lights, who does not change like shifting shadows." God won't be good in a way you'll like today, but then tomorrow be a little sketchy.

"For I know the plans I have for you," declares the LORD, "plans to prosper you and not to harm you, plans to give you hope and a future."

The childlike faith that Jesus tells us is the antidote to the fall of humankind is based on a God who is determined to do good and needed things for us, a God who's trustworthy with the life we actually live.

This was my challenge yesterday, right? I had to make a decision about an organizational problem, but it was overwhelming to predict the consequences of my decision. The problem was a hard one—if it had been simple, I wouldn't have stressed over it. The Psalmist's repeated command to his "self" to praise God in good times and bad times helps us with this. Our own inner selves need to be commanded to do this, because evidently it doesn't come naturally to us. As we do it, we're trusting in the God who works for our good in all things, who invites us to be "more than conquerors" in which bad things not only don't stymie God's good plan for our lives, they get incorporated into those good plans.[52]

But the challenge is believing this, right? Our invitation each day is to "fight the fight of faith,"[53] to take note of whether our hearts are happy in God's promises or are a little, say, cranky. If we're unhappy or overwhelmed, as I was yesterday, our task is again to trust God's work in our actual life by:

- Believing his promises for us, or
- Praising him right in the middle of the thing that stresses us out, or
- Asking him for help and seeing what he does.

---

52 Romans 8:37
53 1 Timothy 6:12

As we live in childlike faith, we come to realize with Philippians 1:25[54] and Romans 15:13[55] that, to our surprise, the barometer of our faith is not, as bounded-set would teach us, our moral uprightness. The barometer of our faith is our level of *joy*. As if God cares about such things!

Now, being human, we'll discover that all of our prayers don't work out the way we hope. Later on, we'll look at what to do with that—which is tied into the "maturity in the midst of childlikeness" that Paul, and the author of Hebrews, were talking about in the quotes earlier.

The faith that Jesus describes falls to the ground if God isn't only good and unyieldingly committed to doing us good all the time, in things that go well and in things that don't.

2. **Our life becomes a childlike journey with Jesus.**

In John 10:27-28, Jesus tells us how we know if we're his "sheep." "My sheep listen to my voice; I know them, and they follow me. I give them eternal life, and they shall never perish; no one will snatch them out of my hand."

This describes a fascinating and surprising dynamic. We're given one standard by which we can know we're his sheep— we listen to his voice! We learn to recognize it, we seek it out, and we rely on it. That's pretty interesting and relational! As we do this, as we look his way throughout our day and listen to him, he *knows* us. This "knowing" is a two-way relationship. Then, as this awesome relationship happens, we realize that he's *moving*—as shepherds do—and so we *follow* him wherever it is that he's going. We want the good pasture and we trust the shepherd to get us there. As we do all of this, we discover that we have eternal life—this dynamic turns out actually to *be* eternal life! As we're listening to and being known by and following alongside this awesome shepherd, we're safe from

---

54 "Convinced of this, I know that I will remain, and I will continue with all of you for your progress and joy in the faith."
55 "May the God of hope fill you with all joy and peace as you trust in him, so that you may overflow with hope by the power of the Holy Spirit."

wolves—we'll never perish and no one will snatch us out of his hand.

Or, to return to our earlier "child of three in the big city" analogy, we discover that our loving parent is walking somewhere with us as we hold their hand and follow along.

Grace and I have taken this to heart.

While we both went to a prestigious university, upon graduation, we focused mostly on listening to Jesus' voice and following where he led us, even as most of our friends were going onto graduate school and professions. When I met Grace, she was living among poor Southeast Asian immigrants in a tenement in San Francisco's Tenderloin District. I—having also felt directed by Jesus to live in a high crime neighborhood for a bit—was writing plays and working entry level jobs. At some point, we got invited to move across the country to try to help start a new church in Massachusetts, which we did after asking God. While we were there, we had five kids as this church—which I ended up pastoring, though that had not been the plan when we moved out there—became a thing. And then, in the middle of its thing-ness, as I've mentioned, we strongly began to wonder if God was calling us into a new adventure another three thousand miles away, one that would require us to rely on God providing for us (my church job had become secure) in ways that he would show us after we made the move.

There are interesting models for this sort of behavior which seem to tie into Jesus' appeal to pursue faith like a child.

Here's one example. In Romans 4, Paul tells us that the best human model of the sort of faith he's talking about is Abraham. This is the guy who got called "the father of all faithful people." Abraham's faith had nothing to do with believing the right stuff or continuing to learn new, esoteric things about theology until he died. It all boiled down to "believing God," as he heard God telling him to move to a mysterious place that he'd be told about later, and as God told him he'd get the biggest dream for his life and have a son and heir even though he and his wife were very old. Abraham's life would be good, even if it endured hardships! Abraham's dreams mattered! Then, Abraham directly lived out the formula that Jesus describes in John 10, this formula that required a journey with the living, on-the-move communicating God.

Abraham's model brings to mind another picture of faith. It's a mythic idea that C.S. Lewis and J.R.R. Tolkien thought and wrote about[56] (and which drove the creation of Lewis's space trilogy and *The Lord of the Rings*). Joseph Campbell picked up on their thoughts in his own way which, several decades later, created the template for *Star Wars*.[57]

Their big idea was that every culture in history seemed to tell two mythic stories—the same stories! (Campbell, as we'll see soon, emphasized one of these.) One was about a dying and rising Harvest God who was buried in winter but brought a harvest in spring. This kept Lewis from following Jesus—after all, wasn't Jesus just one more picture of this Harvest God? On the other hand, Tolkien compellingly argued that Jesus, while very much fitting into this template, was clearly different and more rich and quirky than these other mythic stories. Maybe, he suggested, God implanted the Harvest Myth into all cultures to prepare all cultures for the coming of Jesus, for what he called "myth become fact." Lewis converted that night.

The second universal myth is the interesting one for our purposes. It has many different names. Campbell started out

---

56 In chapters like Lewis's "Myth Become Fact" in *God in the Dock* or J.R.R. Tolkien's "On Fairy Stories" in *Tree and Leaf*, along with passages from Lewis's memoir *Surprised by Joy*.

57 He first discusses this in 1949's *The Hero with a Thousand Faces* (New World Library, 2008). It's super-important and yet, sadly, unreadable. A much more accessible look at Campbell's take on this is Christopher Vogler's *The Writer's Journey: Mythic Structure for Writers* (Michael Wiese, 2007).

by calling it the "monomyth"—the one universal myth, the myth of myths,[58] but it's come to be called the Hero's Journey.

Let's look at its most-basic implications here. The Hero's Journey suggests that each culture has a myth of a small, weak, reluctant hero who gets told they have to leave their safe "ordinary world" (the only world they've known) and will have to enter a scary "special world" which is in fact much bigger and more wonderful and dangerous and mysterious. If they don't take this journey, the world will be destroyed in a great battle that the weak hero didn't even know was already happening. They're often so reluctant to take this journey into this unknown world that they need to be driven out by scary "threshold guardians" or, despite the stakes, they'd never go. In the myth, the reluctant hero often dies mid-journey and needs resurrecting. They need a supernatural guide, as—in the end—there are no human guides for the particular journey they need to take, no ultimate human mentors. (Campbell is a fan of the Galahad story, in which Galahad has to "enter the forest at the darkest point, where no knight has yet gone.") They do save the world in the end, though they then often need to take an arduous return journey back to their ordinary world in which their friends often have no idea what they've just done for the good of everyone and how they've been fundamentally changed as a result.

Perhaps you can imagine how *The Lord of the Rings* or *Star Wars* fit this mold (as do most Hollywood summer blockbusters these days, thanks to the success of Campbell's ideas). But let's think on the question "why would God put this myth into every culture?" If Lewis and Tolkien are onto something that God put the Harvest Myth into every culture in order to prepare the way for humankind to recognize who Jesus was when he showed up, I wonder if God put the Hero's Journey into every culture to tell the story of each of us. What

---

58 He stole the term from *Finnegan's Wake*. He was very into Joyce, whom, along with Picasso, he regarded as one of the great artistic examples of the hero he was talking about.

if we are each the weak, reluctant hero who, nonetheless, is encouraged to leave our ordinary world and embark upon a strange and scary journey into the unexplored special world in order to save the world? Even if we might never be recognized for the amazing thing we've done?

I find this really helpful and explanatory. Abraham's faith fits this template beautifully, for instance. So does the story of Gideon—the weakest member of the weakest tribe of Israel who was cowering in a basement when the angel told him he had to save the world. Or Esther, this nobody who suddenly faced a life or death decision that would either save or destroy everyone she loved.[59] Or Moses with his speech difficulties, who begged God to send someone else. Or the poor fishermen who followed Jesus. Or Rahab the prostitute who saved all of God's people, and on and on. It's as if God put this myth into every culture so we'd have eyes to recognize faith, to recognize spiritual growth when we saw it.

A lot of implications come to mind. It seems to me that, on these terms, the most advice that anyone ever gives anyone else is about how to become king or queen of the ordinary, small world. As if the big story of Frodo Baggins might be how, through cleverness and hard work, he could become mayor of the Shire someday! But the big story for all of us is actually in the vast, unexplored special world, in which we leave behind the latest religious and cultural squabbles in order to take a childlike journey with the Good Shepherd—who, as he did for Abraham, will direct us into a strange land where we'll find the journey we were created to take and where we can save the world—even if nothing there will make us king or queen

---

59 The Hero's Journey can seem pretty male-oriented as it's often presented. Yet Dorothy in *The Wizard of Oz* is an archetypal reluctant hero. Valerie Estelle Frankel devoted a book to seeing the Hero's Journey from a woman's perspective: *From Girl to Goddess: The Heroine's Journey through Myth and Legend* (McFarland & Company, 2010).

in the ordinary world. Abraham, after all, never did become a prosperous landowner in Haran.

It strikes me that anyone whose faith I admire, those I've known or those I've read about, have lived this sort of journey (or still are living this journey). I don't admire them for their "strongly held convictions" or their extensive reading about graduate level religion. I admire them for their childlike faith in a good God who led them to follow his voice into the unknown adventure he'd tailored just for them.

Maybe a month ago, my very guileless son asked me a guileless question. Yes, he was studying hard to be able to get into a decent college engineering program. He liked engineering and it would likely lead to a good job after he graduated—a great thing that's not guaranteed for many college students. But, what if there was more to life? Was his whole life about getting good grades and getting a secure job and hoping to raise a family and go to church and tithe and ultimately die and leave a nice nest egg for his kids? It all felt pressurized and conventional, like he was some kind of sellout.

I wondered if I had two different answers for this, one as a spiritual director and one as a parent. And then maybe I had a way for the stories to converge.

As a spiritual director, of course I was a big fan of the Hero's Journey, of John 10, of childlike faith, of listening for Jesus' voice, doing whatever he said and trusting that this very living, very interactive voice would steer our lives toward a good place. Ever since I faced a very similar crossroads when I was 20 or so, I'd tried to follow that approach to life, right up to the present day. That choice has the advantages of (A) childlikeness, (B) connection to Jesus, (C) unexpected opportunities and (D) a sense that one's life is about big, big, big things—the fate of the whole world, in fact. This is all pretty great stuff and it's the opposite of getting bored looking for meaning from hundreds of sermons (even awesome ones preached by, in just one example, me) and trying to find ways to keep one's faith interesting year in and year out.

However.

This way of life also embraces some real disadvantages, which are worth owning up front. I know no one who has made similar choices who have not found themselves facing some tremendous stress—as Frodo and Luke Skywalker certainly did! My friends have found themselves in financial distress, physical danger and nontrivial existential frustration. Those things have been part of that choice.

As a parent, I wanted to tell my son that, you know, there are worse things than becoming an engineer! Particularly if one enjoys engineering and is good at it! Those "conventional" things that were worrying him had actually been among my greatest joys. I'm really glad God helped me find a wife I like a whole lot. And I really like my kids—him included!—and am so grateful for the resources I can provide for them.

Which of course raises the question about whether these are either/or options. Which, clearly, they're not! Between you and me, I really hope my son gives the engineering thing a try, *and* I hope he lives out John 10 *exactly* like that sheep that Jesus describes. The difference between bounded-set spiritual growth and centered-set spiritual growth is that the first requires constant new information to keep us (marginally) interested, and the other requires all the promise and insecurity of a living relationship that's on the move and might take us to surprising places.

Let's be like Abraham and Esther and Gideon and Rahab and Ruth and Moses and David, and pretty much *every other hero of the Bible* and follow Jesus into the Hero's Journey he has created for us, with all the uncertainty, promise, loneliness, unexpected friendship and possible need for resurrection mid-journey that this childlike, trusting path brings.

3. Childlike faith works, right up until it doesn't.

On the other hand, maybe let's not.

Here's some bad news—particularly disappointing given how far you've had to read before getting it. Most people find

childlike trust in a loving and powerful God to be impossible
to hold onto.

This is obvious, right? Maybe, like me, you had a wonderful,
encouraging first connection with Jesus. He was so present
and eager to answer your prayers, to encourage you and to
speak with you. You realized that this changed everything,
that nothing would ever be the same again, that you'd
follow this amazing and good and loving and personal and
communicative God until the day you died! What you'd
stumbled into, like the man in the field in Jesus' parable, was
un-fricking-believable.

Then, a prayer you prayed with great faith that had great
stakes wasn't answered and … the child died, or the job or the
marriage didn't work out. The church people who'd been so
great and so encouraging to you suddenly weren't so great and
encouraging anymore, and in fact now seemed *mean*, closed-
minded, hypocritical or just … awful.

On this theme, here's a dirty secret we pastors often have:
we know a whole lot of former pastors who swear with a great
deal of passion that they'll never pastor again, that they're not
crazy enough to take the kind of abuse they've put up with for
years. They're *done* with that garbage.

I mean, do you *want* to live the life of a Bible hero? Moses's
first pass at the ordinary world actually didn't look so bad—he
got to live in the palace, have servants and live the high life!
He, in fact, *was* King of the Ordinary World! Was his life so
much *better* after he ran in terror to Midian? Or even after he
was driven into the ultimate special world—the unexplored
desert by the ultimate threshold guardians, Pharaoh's armies—
across the ultimate, can't-go-back threshold into the special
world, the only-parted-one-time Red Sea? It seemed like the
next phase of his "journey into the special world" was marked
mostly by grousing followers who considered killing him
a few times and managed to get God—their "supernatural
guide"—mad at them so repeatedly that the story is one long
succession of poisonous snakes and the ground swallowing

people up until it's climaxed by God's vow that, okay fine, now they'll pretty much all die in the desert. Good times!

At least it *ends* well for Moses, and that's the important thing. Oh, that's right, it doesn't! What seems like a trivial mistake of his, he *also* gets to die in the desert! Sign me up for this Hero's Journey, will you? Three cheers for this kind of childlike faith!

Now, in a calmer moment, some of us might concede that he did, in fact, save the world. His people are freed from slavery, and do end up in a long-promised new country. But maybe stories like this help us get a feel for the stakes of this kind of "childlike faith." If the God who would lead us into *this* kind of journey is in fact as transparently good to us as we talked about a couple of points back, maybe we'd be served by a little more thought on how that's so, at least for the long run.

Let's return to the Hero's Journey for a moment. Remember that part about how the weak, reluctant hero often dies mid-journey and so needs to be resurrected? That seems like a blow. Frodo is impaled by Shelob and *almost* dies. Or maybe the better example from that story is Gandalf the Gray, who does *actually* die (dragged to his death by the Balrog) and needs to be resurrected into the more-powerful Gandalf the White.

This part of the story seems to tell us that our journey will require death and resurrection. That the first blush of how awesome Jesus is and how our lives will never be the same won't last. That this initial, innocent enthusiasm has an important role to play, but if we insist on holding onto it, our story will not end well, for us or for those around us.

Here's a completely fascinating perspective on this from a French philosopher named Paul Ricoeur. He suggests another way of looking at this death and resurrection that we learn about in the Hero's Journey. He calls it "the second naiveté."

Now how Ricoeur uses this and how I'm using it are not one-to-one, but here's the central idea. When we first experience Jesus, we're plunged into the first naiveté. Whatever anyone says about the Bible is awesome. Whatever insights we get in our own scripture readings or prayers are fantastic. Jesus begins to talk to us, and it's astounding. We're confident there are only good things in store for us in this amazing journey of faith we've just been invited onto!

But then, Ricoeur says, we enter "critical distance." We realize that things we'd innocently assumed to be true just don't hold up, either because we get a little learning about the Bible and churches, because we get pushback from smart people, or because life itself doesn't work out the way we thought it would. Our expectations have been messed with.

At this point we have options. One powerful urge would tell us to stuff critical distance at all costs! Go back to the first naiveté! Ignore all that stuff you've been hearing or the experiences you've been having! All those insights about life aren't really worth having if they cost you the first naiveté! Do what you can to crawl back into the womb! In hopes of regaining the safety and security that we've lost, the price we pay when we make this choice is a sort of permanent opposition to everything that called us into critical distance. We become combative, religious people, "standing firm" against challenges from … well, from those lousy people who are experiencing critical distance.

Or, we could camp out in critical distance and become profoundly reactive to combative, religious people. That's another option.

But our goal is the second naiveté, which is this resurrection that the Hero's Journey includes. The second naiveté is the "childlike maturity" that Paul is talking about in 1 Corinthians 13, or the author of Hebrews is talking about in chapter 5. Our goal is to become Gandalf the White. Yoda is both mature *and* childlike. Almost none of us gets this. The road is narrow that leads to life.

Let's circle this again from another perspective. Think back to our earlier discussion of the Garden of Eden. What if, in the Garden before the fall, we're in the first naiveté? God is awesome, the world is awesome and we're wide-eyed with wonderment. But, after the fall, we get expelled from the Garden into critical distance. We'd love to go back to the first naiveté, to the womb, to the happy Garden, to wide-eyed innocence! We feel a horrible sense of loss, yet it's impossible to go back. The entryway to the Garden is guarded by an angel with a flaming sword. We can't go back. Again, if we insist upon, against all hope, demanding to return to that first innocence, I suppose we can camp out right at the gate. Though this, again, will come at the cost of becoming a combative, religious person who has the form of the religion that once meant so much to us, but not the joyful substance. We can't go back in.

Or we can camp out east of Eden, in critical distance. We can recognize that we've come to a place that's hard, that's left us jaded, but can comfort ourselves that at least our eyes have been opened. All that phony-baloney first naiveté stuff is bunk!

But maybe the road rarely taken is to walk around the whole, fallen world—with Jesus as our good shepherd! There will be so much hardship that we experience on this journey! But then, just maybe, we'll see an intriguing, vaguely-familiar sight in front of us. As we get closer, we'll realize it's, hang on, the Garden of Eden! But, having traversed the whole world on this journey with Jesus, we're now entering it from the rear. There's no angel with a flaming sword at *this* gate. As we reenter from the other side, suddenly we've entered into the second naiveté,[60] into transformed resurrection.

This is so helpful.

On so many, ever-deepening levels.

Here's a story or two. When I first started following Jesus, as I said, the whole experience was amazing. God spoke to me, I saw a whole lot of powerful prayers answered, and I

---

60 This leaving-Eden-and-traveling-around-the-whole-world-until-you-reenter-it-from-the-rear perspective was suggested by M. Scott Peck in *Further Along the Road Less Traveled: The Unending Journey Towards Spiritual Growth* (Touchstone, 1993).

found friends who joyfully studied the Bible with me. I loved it! At the time, my passion was to write plays or novels. And I did—only to enter a cycle of rising expectations followed by devastating reversals. My first play was fought over by two different theater groups at my prestigious university—including the school's drama department. This was unprecedented. I got press attention. Major theatre companies from around the country were keeping an eye on this acclaimed, promising young playwright. It appeared I was—thanks to Jesus!—about to be launched quite prominently into my biggest dream.

And then, for a variety of reasons, the production never happened and I entered into fifteen years—fifteen years!—of working entry-level jobs as I tried to get back to that opportunity.

Some years later, after my life took a very different turn and I pastored a church, I sublimated my playwriting hopes into novel-writing. After one unsuccessful attempt, I secured a prestigious literary agent with my second. This was a big deal. I read a statistic that, for every four hundred novels written, only one gets agented, and this wasn't just any agent—she'd just represented a number one *New York Times* bestseller. And she was into my book. When we met in Manhattan, she said the main questions for me to consider were how I wanted to handle foreign rights and movie rights. And then she couldn't sell the book and—with you'll-get-'em-next-time regret—she dropped me. Even after finding another agent and writing another novel, with that agent's strong guidance, I remain an unpublished novelist to this day.[61]

On the upside, I saw some remarkable success in helping start a church and seeing it become prominent and newsworthy. However, like all of my closest pastor friends, I've experienced my share of mean—sometimes persistent—attacks, often from people who'd been friends.

---

61 One of my novels did get a boutique publication, but that's another story.

My baby daughter was desperately sick to the point of being given only a tiny chance of survival—and then, as thousands of great people fasted and prayed for her recovery, she completely recovered and is a vibrant young woman as I write this. Then, only a couple of years later, one of my closest friends—a young man, quite a beloved husband and father and pastor—discovered he had stage 4 colon cancer and *also* was prayed for by thousands of great people and nonetheless died a horrible, wasting death at exactly the time his doctors predicted he'd die.

I could go on. Of course I could. Because I've lived many decades of life since that first, amazing encounter with Jesus. And you might have stories that would put to shame my stories here.

So what does childlike faith look like at this stage of life? What does it look like to enter the second naiveté, to travel through the whole, fallen world as we follow our very good shepherd, Jesus?

In that spirit, let me sum it up.

The childlike faith that Jesus invites us into turns out to involve two and only two things:

- It involves keeping our hearts happy and open-hearted in God, even as life happens.

- It involves an ongoing journey of faith.

But how, specifically, do you pull that off on your journey to the second naiveté? I think the key is that, however you do those two things, you do them. There are many great models. But, if only as one example, here are a few things I do.

- **I fight the fight of faith daily.**

Early each day, I note whether my heart seems happy in God's promises. If not, my day's task becomes getting to that place. That might happen as I praise God right in the midst of the problems that are making me anxious, or as I pray or claim promises from the Bible, or as Grace or another friend prays for me. But I do this.

- **I give time to listen to Jesus' voice as best as I can.**

This is in the spirit of John 10. The seminal book that talks about this is Brother Lawrence's *The Practice of the Presence of God.* As I mentioned, I often talk with God as I walk. Grace gets distracted on walks, so she starts many of her days with a journal as she writes out her dialogue with God. And then I'm eager to follow whatever counsel or direction Jesus gives me. It's super helpful.

- **I'm diligent to forgive and break off curses.**

On the days when my distress comes from what, to me, feels like judgment from other people, I'm quick to take time to forgive them and then to break off the curse of their judgment.[62]

They may, of course, accurately see some bad quality in me. Nonetheless, Jesus commands us never to judge[63] and I find I'm not strong enough to carry the feeling of being judged by even one person, so I spiritually break the curse of each judgment I feel. If I find myself stewing over how badly I've been treated by a person I've just forgiven (and whose judgments I just broke off), I repeat the process until I'm no longer stewing over them and have released them.

I do stuff like that. And lots of other stuff like reading the Bible or getting together with friends and praying for each other and going to worship services and many more things.

I'm sure you have your own ways of returning to a heart that's happy in God's good promises over your life even as you follow Jesus into your own, Abraham-like journey into the special world.

Now it can be a lot of fun to learn interesting, new theological truths! If you want to get a graduate theological degree, please don't let me stop you! But the stuff of growth is the stuff of the living, interactive journey with the God who

---

62 Proverbs 26:2. "Like a fluttering sparrow or a darting swallow,/ an undeserved curse does not come to rest."

63 Matthew 7:1

loves you and is committed to doing good things for you that you very much want. That childlike journey of faith, around the entire sinful world, is the antidote to the fall. Its rewards are profound and transforming. Those rewards are what you've been created to experience and pass on.

I'm praying for you.

5

Religious Squabbles Are the Worst (But There's an Antidote!)

I didn't grow up in the churchgoing club. That turned out to matter.

AS WE'VE TALKED about, I entered faith in Jesus from outside of the churchgoing club. This made for some rip-roaring early discussions with Grace. She started following Jesus—quite intentionally—when she was five years old. She grew up in the Bible Belt, and judged her mainline church's Sunday school, and her youth group, as not being serious enough about God.

So for instance. We were sitting on our floral couch in front of our picture windows on a sunny morning as—serious Christians that we were—we connected about our thoughts on the Bible passages we'd read that morning. I talked about how powerful my experience reading Genesis 2 and 3 had been. But Grace was troubled by some of my language. "Hold on, hold on, hold on," she said. "Are you implying you don't believe that there was an actual Adam and Eve?"

My training was in literature. I said, tentatively, that, to my mind, the Garden of Eden story didn't need to be literal to be profound, helpful and true. She scowled, so I resumed backpedaling. "Look," I said, "surely whoever wrote these chapters …" More scowling. "I mean, right, tradition says it was Moses. So, fine, let's say it was Moses. Can we agree that

Moses wasn't an eyewitness to this story? I don't think it's controversial to say that he wrote this by way of oral tradition, right? Of hearing stories passed down for hundreds of years? So he's not passing on a transcript of, like, what God said to Adam and Eve. And, while we're on that subject, should we note that 'Adam' means 'the man' and 'Eve' means 'life' or 'Mother of All Living?' Does that seem suggestive to you? Is the author—Moses! I'm sure it was Moses!—trying to tell us something about who we are as people? About why the world is the way it is? It seems to me that the rest of the Bible builds on the insights in these two chapters and that they're among the deepest and most useful stories ever written, that they're as true as true can be. It's entirely possible that in the next life we'll discover that, what do you know?, the world was indeed created in seven 24-hour days and this actual guy named Adam named all the animals and this actual woman named Eve was indeed literally created from one of his ribs one night and that God said exactly what he's recorded as saying here. If that's the case, no problem! All I'm saying is that the power and helpfulness of these chapters doesn't, to me, rest on those things. And we seem to be given lots of hints that suggest a different purpose to what the author—Moses!—is trying to do."

After a long pause, I asked Grace what she was thinking. "Thanks for asking," she said. "What I'm thinking is 'I can't believe I married a heretic!'"

Now she said it with a twinkle in her eye and our discussions to follow were only encouraging and fun, for reasons I'll elaborate on below. But we'd seen very different things when we'd looked at those same passages.

As someone who entered the Jesus thing from outside of the churchgoing bounded set, I saw lots of early examples of differing perceptions.

In my first-ever church service, the conservative megachurch was—per Matthew 18—excommunicating a leader for his (they said) unrepentant adultery. In the spirit of "taking [this man's sin] to the church," they put his phone number on the screen and encouraged us all to call him and urge him to repent. Afterwards I asked my friend if this happened often in the church. No! he said. This was super-rare and I should come back the next week. I had another question: Was I, a visitor who was only just considering this God stuff, supposed to call this man? No, my friend said, that was only for the members.

So the next week I went back and they preached about how women weren't allowed to teach men, per 1 Timothy 2:12.[64] I had another interesting conversation with my friend on that drive home. I mean, I knew lots of really smart, accomplished women. Whenever I listened to them tell me about fascinating things they knew, was I—Satan-like—tempting them to sin?

A reminder: we're talking about Blue Ocean's six distinctives.

Just to re-situate you at this stage of the book.

1. Our primary framework is SOLUS JESUS.

2. Our primary metaphor is CENTERED-SET.

3. Our approach to spiritual development is CHILDLIKE FAITH.

4. Our approach to controversial issues is THIRD WAY.

5. Our approach to other churches is ECUMENICAL.

6. Our approach to secular culture is JOYFUL ENGAGEMENT.

   Okay. Onward!

Maybe we're helped by looking at more than one perspective on religious squabbles.

Squabbles like this might seem … I don't know … charming to you. Or not. But these and similar squabbles prove to be a big deal indeed in terms of how Christians relate to one

---

64 "I do not permit a woman to teach or to assume authority over a man; she must be quiet."

another. The markers we use when we discuss Christianity's history are customarily when big, unresolvable disputes happened. The Orthodox Church split from Rome in 1054. The Protestant Reformation hit in 1517. And so on. As I write this, churches are in a cage fight about the place of LGBT people. In my relatively brief time of following Jesus, similar fights have happened around whether divorced and remarried people can have full standing in a church, or—per the anecdote above—whether women can preach.

I have many thoughts on what the misfire is in conversations like these. I'm not sure which one is right.

Maybe the misfire is cultural. Again, I hadn't grown up in the same settings as the folks who ran the church I visited. My background was secular. These folks were very churched. It was hard for them not to see those differences as entirely my problem. After all, their culture was God's culture! If— as seemed true to them—the scriptures were "clear" on any areas in dispute, well, that should settle it. If I mentioned that my experience of life, and my educational background, would suggest some different grids and perspectives at play in the scriptures we were talking about, some perspectives that perhaps they hadn't considered, they might bring up that a huge fallacy (and sin!) was letting the hostile, secular culture influence my practice of faith. You might recognize a bounded/centered-set conflict at play here.

Maybe Stage Theory has something to offer us.

I discovered another way to look at this that really helped me.

It was a four-stage perspective on emotional and spiritual development[65] proposed by psychologist M. Scott Peck,

---

65 Psychologists just love stage theories of development, so Peck's is one of many. You might be familiar with similar theories from Maslow or from a Christian like James Fowler. Also, it's not just psychologists. I know of one from Catholic spiritual direction, so let me affirm the wonderful value of whichever is your favorite! For our purposes here, I find Peck's really helpful.

who wrote a 1980s bestseller on related themes called *The Road Less Traveled*. In a later speech, he wondered if human emotional and spiritual development would each progress through four different developmental stages in a perfectly healthy, non-traumatized person.[66] The dilemma was that we all went through trauma, some of which could keep us from further progress. What was most useful to him was how these stages might explain why we miss each other and so engage in endless, hopeless conflicts.

Stage 1 you might call "criminal."

It corresponds with being a toddler. Toddlers don't entirely know where they end and you begin, and so they're prone to being grabby and self-focused. It's not their fault—they're toddlers! I have children, and I can say with confidence that I've never arrived home to find a toddler melting down because another sibling was denying them a favorite toy, who then was able to miraculously pull themselves together, stop crying, look at me, and say, "But, Daddy, it's not all about me. How was your day?"

Peck suggests two institutions that interact with this stage: jail and the boardroom (or any other position of power). Jail serves Stage 1 people, because it provides clear boundaries— the bars of the cell if nothing else. High-functioning Stage 1 people can also become the kind of effective narcissists that get power because you and I don't realize that they're criminals doing everything for their own gain. Think Bernie Madoff. Or Stalin.

---

66 This was published in *Further Along the Road Less Traveled: The Unending Journey Towards Spiritual Growth* (Touchstone, second edition, 1998). It's in chapter 7, a transcript of a speech he gave as president of the American Psychological Association, called "Spirituality and Human Nature."

Stage 2 you might call "rules-based."

Now we're six or seven and we want to obey Mommy and Daddy's rules. Peck suggests two institutions which serve and promote Stage 2. First is the military, which is famously excellent at transitioning young people out of Stage 1 and into Stage 2, at teaching them discipline and honor and making them productive citizens. Second—of greater interest for our purposes— are churches. Peck argues that churches (and mosques, synagogues and other places of worship) famously teach people right from wrong, good from bad. He's at pains not to judge this, pointing out that Stage 2 creates the backbone of most societies. It creates the good people who volunteer, pay taxes, obey the law and raise great kids.

If I can go global for a moment, a friend of mine has given a lot of thought to the stages as they map out over world history. He grew up in a third world country, and he told me that the most important transition in societies is between Stages 1 and 2, which happens when a given country gets the rule of law. It's a pretty big deal to be able to walk down one's street at night in safety, or to trust that the leaders of one's country, while perhaps self-interested, are not Stage 1 criminals looting the treasury.

Stage 3 you might call "rebellious."

This corresponds with being a teenager. Suddenly the Stage 3 person is asking, "Who died and made all those Stage 2 rules the rules?" They become skeptics. If the Stage 3 young person is surrounded by a Stage 2 community, they might feel suffocated. Where's the open questioning? Are all these Stage 2 "truths" just shallow grabs for power? Peck says the institution that best promotes Stage 3 is the university. For one thing, universities are filled with kids in this age range, and often their stated mission is quite Stage 3—to get students to question everything they've been taught.

It seems to me that whole communities—or even countries—can stereotypically fit into these stages. Clearly, each place has people throughout the spectrum of the stages. But perhaps a single stage dominates the cultural perception of a given area. So Grace's childhood home, in the Bible Belt, would be stereotypically Stage 2. France might be stereotypically Stage 3. A war-torn country might be stereotypically Stage 1. Places that I've lived in, like heavily-educated Cambridge, Massachusetts, would neatly fit into Stage 3.

Per our conversation in this chapter, Stages 2 and 3 mostly fight. Stage 2 looks at Stage 3 as lawbreakers, as bad people who think the rules don't apply to them. Hence the Bible Belt's denunciation of "the Eastern, liberal elite." Stage 3 usually looks down on Stage 2 people as buffoons, as stupid. To them, Stage 2 people seem unable to entertain that they prefer a black and white world that doesn't require actual thought. So Stage 3 responds to Stage 2 with a sneer.[67] I wonder if Twitter and Facebook controversies are mostly Stage 2 versus Stage 3 squabbles, in an endless dance.

What Stage 3 doesn't realize is that its skepticism might not be the final word, that there might actually be answers to its questions, but answers that look quite different than the answers proposed by Stage 2.

Stage 4 you might call "mystical."

Stage 4, in Peck's view, isn't the end of the process. At the earliest, we hit this stage in our early 20s, and then we spend the rest of our lives walking out the implications of this. In Stage 4 we realize that many of the things that we were taught in Stage 2 do, in fact, seem true, but in a more expansive perspective than we'd previously understood. So, for instance, take a Christian truism like, "Believe in Jesus and be saved." In Stage 2, we might say, "Well, at 3 p.m. yesterday I did believe in Jesus, so I can write in my journal that, whatever else may

---

67 Back to the last chapter, you might look at Stage 2 as people trying to return to the first naiveté, camping out at the gate. Stage 3 would be people in critical distance.

happen in my life, now I know for sure that I'm going to heaven." That may be entirely true, but in Stage 4, you might instead find yourself saying, "Wow! I think I do believe in Jesus! This is amazing! I never knew this kind of connection with God—and with myself and the world around me—was possible! How do I keep believing in Jesus in just this way, day in and day out, year in and year out? And 'saved'—clearly if this means I'll get to go to heaven, I'm all in! But it feels like I'm being saved right now! What does it look like to keep that going?"

Think back to our discussion of childlike faith, which talked about the dynamics of a childlike trust in a communicative God and what such a faith would look like as it faced all the challenges that all lives face. A central scripture for this might come from Jesus, in John 10. "My sheep listen to my voice; I know them, and they follow me. I give them eternal life, and they shall never perish; no one will snatch them out of my hand." Now, on the one hand, entering Stage 4 offers a kind of maturing that you can't find in any other stage. Stage 4 is just a starting point, is endlessly expansive and is growth-central.[68] In Stage 4, you do, as I've said, suddenly realize that the most useful Stage 2 rules *point to* something—and that last part is what's actually helpful and interesting.[69] But the mechanism

---

68 You could make a case that Stage 4 equates either with the second naiveté, or with being on the road towards the second naiveté.

69 My friend and partner on the Blue Ocean World podcast, Tom Wassink, puts it this way as he reads this paragraph: For me, the Sermon on the Mount statements by Jesus: "You have heard it said…, but I say…" are explicit Stage 4 reinterpretations of Stage 2 rules. Jesus is not abandoning the rules, but describing the deeper reality that they point to, that they are referencing. So Jesus doesn't say, "Those are dumb rules, and rules are by nature dumb," but rather, "Pay attention to what the rules are pointing towards." Or, to me, another classic Stage 4 moment is when Jesus and the disciples pick grain and eat it on the Sabbath, are challenged by the Pharisees, and Jesus says, "Man is not made for the Sabbath, but the Sabbath for man." Rules are for

for this maturing remains a sort of childlikeness. Stick with me, and I think you'll get a sense of why that's so.

One way to think about this is that Stage 2 is dominated by *answers*. If the key is to be a good person and to get things right, we need to know what is and isn't right. In a Christian world, it might take some work to know what you need to know about the Bible. You might need to read not just the Bible, but the current favorite Christian thinker of your friends. But, after you've done this, you're good. Maybe you won't know everything, but you'll have the answers you need.

Stage 4, though, is dominated by *questions*. You've realized that reality is way bigger than you are, and that the way to navigate its vastness is relational. You are the sheep listening to and following the good shepherd. This will make Stage 4 Christians seem slippery to Stage 2 Christians. They seem to use the same language, but they mean different things with it.

Imagine three stick figures.

Maybe a stick figure diagram can help us.[70] The first stick figure has a circle above its head. The circle represents Truth. Call this "Primitive People." Primitive people believed that there was truth out there, but they didn't have access to it, and so they needed shamans, mediums or primitive priests to help connect them to that truth, to bring it down to where it could help them.

The second has a circle about the same size as the stick figure itself. Call this "Stage 2 People." (Or, if you're into thinking historically, you might call this "Modern People.") Now we realize that, while Truth is out there, thanks to the scientific method and good thinking, it's about the same size as we are. It will, yes, take some work to explore it, but it's very do-able. Truth is about the same size as we are.

---

our benefit, meant to serve us. We are not meant to be *ruled* by them, but to be over them and administrate them with the ultimate goal of fruitfulness.

70 Thanks to Andrew Snekvik for this.

The third has a massive circle with a tiny stick figure just inside of it. Call this "Stage 4 People." As Stage 4 people, we realize we've just popped through a bubble into this vast, amazing world of Truth. It's huge! Way bigger than we are! The good news is that, as we traverse this vast circle throughout the rest of our lives, we have no hope of making our way across it—it's just too big. But wherever we look—in front of us, behind us, over our heads, wherever—we'll only see truth. The truth is everywhere. It surrounds us.[71]

Not everyone loves stage theory.

Stage theory is the greatest. It's so useful. But, I have cautions. I can confirm that some people find it elitist. If they feel targeted as Stage 2 people, they understandably feel an intrinsic pressure that—given that these stages are numbered—they're being told they're not as hip or worthy as those in the later stages. Anticipating this, Peck emphasizes that these stages are mostly useful as we consider why we end up in unresolvable conflicts, that there are strengths in each stage (even Stage 1, where we are in touch with what we actually want) and that, as we continue on through the stages, we don't leave the earlier stages behind, but instead add to them. I vividly remember an early experience of teaching this to a large group of mostly twenty-something people. After the talk, I heard several of them animatedly holding court at tables in the lobby. They loved this! *This* explained why they had such a hard time with their family and with their churches—they were Stage 4 and the others were Stage 2! This was so helpful! Of course, what I was thinking was that their conversations were telling me they were in fact Stage *3*—living in reaction to their conservative upbringing and using stage theory to put words to the superiority they felt. But, all that said, it's still true

---

71 This is from G.K. Chesterton in *Orthodoxy*. "The poet [or "Stage 4 person"] only asks to get his head into the heavens. It is the logician [or "Stage 2 person"] who seeks to get the heavens into his head. And it is his head that splits."

that this says that each subsequent stage is a step of growth and that can feel hard if we identify with an earlier stage.

Now, onto the good stuff.

Religious squabbles tend to be fights between stages 2, 3 and 4. As I mentioned, in the public sphere, they're almost always between stages 2 and 3, with Stage 4 watching as onlookers (usually cheering on Stage 3, but recognizing the limitations of the solutions their Stage 3 friends are promoting). The Stage 2, rules-keeping impulse will always be to say, "But the Bible is clear on my position! There's no further conversation to be had unless you want to abandon the Bible—in which case there's *also* no further conversation to be had!" Again, the Stage 2 person will customarily feel that their Stage 3, rebellious antagonist has "capitulated to secular culture"—that their theological enemy has shamefully given in to their craving to be regarded as cool by the hostile, godless world. What else could explain their disagreement with the "clear" truth of the Bible that all of the Stage 2 person's other friends regard as obvious? It must be a moral failing. The Stage 3 person will be exasperated that their Stage 2 antagonist doesn't seem capable of having an actual conversation about the stakes of the conversation, but relies on name-calling and intransigence. If the Stage 3 person is a Christian, they'll feel that they've deeply considered the same scriptures that the Stage 2 person has only looked at in passing before locking into their belligerence.

"Soft" and "hard" stages.

Reflecting on our conversation over the Adam and Eve story in Genesis, Grace would now say that it helped her discover that in many ways she was "soft Stage 2." This meant that she'd only ever been in Stage 2 Christian settings, so she had never considered other alternatives of how to look at the stories we were discussing. But also that she wasn't in any way committed to the trappings of Stage 2, unlike the combative "hard Stage 2" people who love the certainty and safety of Stage

2, but defend *that*—rather than Jesus—to the death. Grace just wanted to know Jesus better. If anything could help her in that, it was all good to her, if initially jarring. By contrast, perhaps the leaders of the conservative megachurch I'd visited would present as hard Stage 2.

Perhaps there are also hard and soft Stage 3 people. Soft Stage 3 people would be skeptics, but open to truth and growth wherever they can find it. Hard Stage 3 people would be committed to skepticism and anti-religious sneering, no matter what new information came their way.

To mention one more challenging dynamic in conflicts between these stages, it seems that many Stage 2 people, understandably, only believe there is one other stage—Stage 1. This can lead to them treating every opponent as Stage 1, as an out-of-control criminal. Hence their tendency to condescension and shaming in these fights. Not having experienced Stage 3 or Stage 4, they can't imagine other alternatives than being either a rules keeper or a rules breaker.

The starting point: We're doomed.

Here's our question: Are religious squabbles fated to go badly, because they're usually conducted by people coming from different stages? If you and your debate opponent don't share the same way of looking at the world (or at God or at humanity), maybe there's no way these squabbles can be resolved.

Let's use a current case study. I mentioned a moment ago that, as I write this, the hot religious controversy is about the place for LGBT people in churches.

When we were at the very start of our church in Cambridge, I met a thoughtful young woman who was an out lesbian, which was still a bold choice in an evangelical church at the time. I asked her if I could buy her coffee and pick her brain for a few minutes.

We had a wonderful conversation that ended on a sobering note.

I'd long had a feeling that a black mark on most Christianity was how it treated gay, lesbian and transgender people. I knew many stories of sincere LGBT people who hoped to follow God with a given church, and ultimately felt driven out. That seemed crazy to me, and I wondered if my new acquaintance would have any advice for me.

She did. "Your church will never help LGBT people, Dave," she said. "I'll tell you that right now. I might be an exception, although even I can't claim that I'll last with you. [She didn't. I saw her maybe once more.] Look, I believe you that you want to be helpful to LGBT people, and to invite us to follow Jesus alongside you. But you're embedded in a system that's a lot more repressive than you realize. So I'm saying you're naïve. Unless you completely start over, this is a settled conversation."

A lot of cultures were at work in my conversation with this woman.

One was my own culture. Having grown up secular, it had always been a mystery to me why gay people couldn't follow Jesus alongside straight people. So, even early on in my pastoral career in an evangelical church movement, I was pressing an unpopular issue. I was aware of the scriptures in play in this dispute, and my read on them was quite different than that of my conservative friends. And perhaps you can see how my (at that point) newfound fascination with centered-set would play in. If the whole ballgame in centered-set faith was pointing our own arrows Jesus' direction, and encouraging others to do that as well, then doing this would be a good thing—the ultimate good thing—for all people, from all cultures, gay or straight. It seemed jarring to me to exclude groups of people from this.

One was evangelical culture. My friends who'd grown up as regular churchgoers in conservative churches didn't remotely come at this from my perspective. They were aware of the six or seven verses in the Bible that seemed hostile to homosexuality and those seemed conclusive to them. Why I'd even ask the question seemed mysterious and unsettling. Had I read those verses? I'd read them, right?

Another was this woman's culture. As someone who'd worshipped in conservative churches, she was aware in ways that I wasn't of the barriers to LGBT people being supported and embraced by those churches. Much as she might like me personally, it was hard—even painful—for her even to talk openly with a pastor of a church in an evangelical denomination.

On stage theory terms, we seem doomed here. What seems to one culture to be a justice issue is seen by another culture as a holiness issue. Having had hundreds of hours of conversations on this, I have data on how this conversation goes. Among soft Stage 2 and Stage 3 friends, it goes great. It's challenging and painstaking and doesn't move quickly, but we find lots of common ground and hear each other out and look at the Bible together and the conversation does progress.

But the public debate is conducted by people in hard Stage 2 and hard Stage 3. We're told either that "liberals" are godless appeasers who don't care about the teachings of the Bible or that "conservatives"[72] are bigots who will answer for their sins on judgment day. This particular conversation likely *is* hopeless because each side, with the agenda set by the intransigent members of their camp, is dug into their stage. Knowing the stories of many churches that have engaged this issue, this absolutely is the way it tends to go.

Yes, over time, the wider culture does tend to force these issues forward. To most of my evangelical friends, the thought that women shouldn't be permitted to preach seems crazy, while it was mainstream in their circles a quarter century ago. Among evangelical youth, support for gay rights is quickly rising. So these fights are eventually resolved. However, in the moment, while I'll suggest a way forward, let's not kid

---

72 In quotation marks because, in my experience, neither side embraces these labels, at least as applied to themselves.

ourselves. Most religious squabbles, in the short term, are destined for an unwinnable war for just these reasons.

Saint Paul would like to interject a thought.

Feel free to push back on this, but as I scan the Bible, it seems to me that the savviest thinker on cultural issues is Paul. He grew up in one culture—one bounded set—and it took one of the most famous supernatural conversion stories in recorded literature to jolt him into a centered set. Suddenly, he was learning from another, very different culture. For the rest of his life, he reflected quite a lot about the difficulties that different cultures have in working through their different perspectives. He's the guy who argued that among Jesus' most important, most central miracles was "breaking dividing walls" between cultures.[73] To Paul, doing this one thing was Jesus'

---

73 He argued this most directly in Ephesians, which a whole lot of scholars—many of them conservative—don't think he wrote, so there's that. If he didn't write it, it was likely written by one or more people "in his school," who regard themselves as representing Paul's point of view. So perhaps attributing some of these sentiments to him isn't crazy talk. Here are a few key verses on this subject: "For he himself is our peace, who has made the two groups one and has destroyed the barrier, the dividing wall of hostility, by setting aside in his flesh the law with its commands and regulations. His purpose was to create in himself one new humanity out of the two, thus making peace, and in one body to reconcile both of them to God through the cross, by which he put to death their hostility" (2:14-16). He's talking specifically here about the massive division between the Jews (his birth culture) and the Gentiles (everybody other than the Jews, mostly Greek-born in his experience). Maybe we should just regard this as applying to this one cultural division and not make it represent all cultural divisions. The central scripture we'll be considering, from Romans 14, also focuses on a Jew-Gentile fight, but we find suspicious parallels with other cultural squabbles here. For instance, in this passage, we have conservative "defenders of the Bible" standing their ground against the godless hordes assailing them, hordes that—with Paul now in their

in-your-face "to the rulers and authorities in the heavenly realms."[74]

Paul's most pointed message on the subject comes in Romans 14. (Remember that this is not a scriptural look at the issue we're using as an example—LGBT inclusion in churches. It's a scriptural look at how to have such conversations in the middle of profound disagreement.) Here's the whole chapter:

> Accept the one whose faith is weak, without quarreling over disputable matters. One person's faith allows them to eat anything, but another, whose faith is weak, eats only vegetables. The one who eats everything must not treat with contempt the one who does not, and the one who does not eat everything must not judge the one who does, for God has accepted them. Who are you to judge someone else's servant? To their own master, servants stand or fall. And they will stand, for the Lord is able to make them stand.

> One person considers one day more sacred than another; another considers every day alike. Each of them should be fully convinced in their own mind. Whoever regards one day as special does so to the Lord. Whoever eats meat does so to the Lord, for they give thanks to God; and whoever abstains does so to the Lord and gives thanks to God. For none of us lives for ourselves alone, and none of us dies for ourselves alone. If we live, we live for the Lord; and if we die, we die for the Lord. So, whether we live or die, we belong to the Lord. For this very reason, Christ died and returned to

---

ranks—nonetheless seem to feel that they have a needed vantage point on the scriptures that the conservative defenders haven't seen.

74 Ephesians 3:10

life so that he might be the Lord of both the dead
and the living.

You, then, why do you judge your brother or
sister? Or why do you treat them with contempt?
For we will all stand before God's judgment seat.
It is written:

"'As surely as I live,' says the Lord, 'every knee will
bow before me; every tongue will acknowledge
God.'"

So then, each of us will give an account of
ourselves to God.

Therefore let us stop passing judgment on one
another. Instead, make up your mind not to put
any stumbling block or obstacle in the way of a
brother or sister. I am convinced, being fully
persuaded in the Lord Jesus, that nothing is
unclean in itself. But if anyone regards something
as unclean, then for that person it is unclean. If
your brother or sister is distressed because of
what you eat, you are no longer acting in love. Do
not by your eating destroy someone for whom
Christ died. Therefore do not let what you know
is good be spoken of as evil. For the kingdom of
God is not a matter of eating and drinking, but
of righteousness, peace and joy in the Holy Spirit,
because anyone who serves Christ in this way is
pleasing to God and receives human approval.

Let us therefore make every effort to do what
leads to peace and to mutual edification. Do not
destroy the work of God for the sake of food. All
food is clean, but it is wrong for a person to eat
anything that causes someone else to stumble. It
is better not to eat meat or drink wine or to do

anything else that will cause your brother or sister to fall.

So whatever you believe about these things keep between yourself and God. Blessed is the one who does not condemn himself by what he approves. But whoever has doubts is condemned if they eat, because their eating is not from faith; and everything that does not come from faith is sin.

In this chapter, Paul thinks he's helping us all avoid quarrelling over "disputable matters." But, of course, the trick is to figure out which fights are actually "disputable" by reasonable people—whatever is the current hot controversy often feels life-and-death in the moment, feels a long way from being disputable. You might say that allowing divorced-and-then-remarried people to lead in your church is disputable; I might say it's a clear outrage.[75] Therein lies our problem.

Paul anticipates this question in a number of ways.

His examples of disputable matters in his own day might seem trivial to modern readers. A key dispute of his era was about whether faithful believers could eat meat sacrificed to idols. Most likely you haven't run across that moral dilemma. In Rome, however, all meat was sacrificed to Roman gods as it was being butchered. This was no minor deal to faithful Jews. A large swath of the Hebrew Bible talked about the centrality of keeping oneself pure, of not being contaminated by the evils of the pagan neighboring countries. This was about as big of an issue to observant Jews as you could find. The entirely holy God spoke out quite directly about spiritual adultery, but Gentile converts to Jesus felt no such compunction. They didn't have that history. To them, whatever ritual the butchers did over the meat meant nothing. The conservatives in this dispute, mostly made up of observant Jews, had a simple solution—just do what we say, eat only vegetables, and we'll all

---

75 I wouldn't, in fact, say that.

be good. But, Paul himself could never agree to that, because that would mean that the gospel had become cultural. One culture had to adopt another culture in order to know God, which would deny that God was a God of the whole world. A challenging problem!

His other example also might seem trivial to modern readers: "considering one day more sacred than another." What are we talking about here, moon festivals? Who cares! Well, if the day in question is the Sabbath day, that's a pretty big deal to observant Jews, one of the Ten Commandments in fact.

The issues he's chosen aren't any less difficult than the ones in our day.

Given how hard this is to sort out, let's consider a category distinction that's had some staying power, which was articulated by a theologian named Roger E. Olson.[76] It's the distinction between three types of biblical beliefs.

A key distinction: three types of biblical beliefs

- **Dogma**
- **Doctrine**
- **Opinion**

These theologians understand "dogma" to be the basics of Christian faith, which are statements about who God is, and particularly who Jesus is. The Apostle's and Nicene Creeds would be the most central formulations of Christian dogma. If you differ on these points, you're talking about a different faith than Christianity.

"Doctrine" boils down to what you regard as implications from your dogma. The hot disputes of a given era usually fall into this category. The conservative Jews of Paul's era would regard not eating meat sacrificed to idols as a key implication

---

76 He talks about this in his book *Reformed and Always Reforming: The Postconservative Approach to Evangelical Theology* (Baker Academic, 2007).

of their dogma of who God is. God is perfectly holy and so we, too, must maintain holiness. Not eating this meat would seem quite tied to their view of God, to dogma. The key thing to realize is that it's *tied* to one's dogma, but it is not *itself* the dogma. It's an implication. It's doctrine. Doctrinal disputes tend to be the things that cause Christian movements to splinter.

"Opinion" is everything else. Like everyone I know, I think some worship music is lousy, even though other people like it and seem to be able to worship to it just fine. I recognize that these opinions are just my preferences, but I'm still quite tempted to argue that my preferences are in fact *right*. In fact, I do argue that frequently. There's nothing wrong with theological opinions so long as we recognize they're not doctrine or, even more importantly, dogma.

Now, of course, the challenge is that people dispute what belongs in each category. The observation over the last hundred and fifty years or so has been that theological conservatives are tempted to call everything dogma, even opinions, and that theological liberals are tempted to call everything opinion, even dogma.

Let's work with this for a moment.

What constitutes a "disputable matter?"

1. It's not a matter of Christian dogma.

Again, we don't want to mess with the Apostle's and Nicene Creeds.[77]

---

77 Unless, like Harvey Cox, in his delightfully provocative, late-period book *The Future of Faith* (HarperOne, 2010) you do in fact want to mess with the Nicene Creed, at the very least. But, for our purposes here, can we agree on dogma about Jesus and the Godhead? We can mix it up over beer later.

2. It brings two biblical truths into dynamic tension.

In the case of meat sacrificed to idols, you could make a case that the two truths were purity and freedom—both major biblical themes.

3. Otherwise faithful believers disagree over it.

By definition, it's a disputable matter when thoughtful Christians in fact dispute it. Now, this doesn't work when talking with hard Stage 2 or hard Stage 3 people. To them, any disagreement means that that the person disagreeing is apostate, and so good will is required here. However, if the person disagreeing with you has seemed like a fellow follower of Jesus—and the dispute doesn't involve Christian dogma— you've just entered into disputable matter territory.

What does Paul advise us to do?

1. By all means hold the beliefs that you hold and never violate your conscience.

"Everyone should be fully convinced in their own mind."

"But those who have doubts are condemned if they eat, because their eating is not from faith; and everything that does not come from faith is sin."

I have beliefs about all of the issues we've talked about in this chapter, and I feel my beliefs are the right ones, or I would have different ones. My beliefs, obviously, have affected how the churches I've led have been run—for instance, women preach in them and I won't baptize a baby because it would go against my conscience.

The key distinction is that any congregant is free to believe differently.

In the membership classes I led, we encouraged each member to be baptized. Despite my anti-infant-baptism belief, if a listener was baptized as an infant and it seemed like baptism to them, that was fine with us, whatever my belief, if only because half of the entire Christian world disagrees with my belief, so clearly, faithful people can differ.

2. Shun contempt and judgment and trust God to judge wisely.

"You, then, why do you judge your brother or sister? Or why do you treat your brother or sister with contempt? For we will all stand before God's judgment seat."

Again, Stage 2 tends to dismiss Stage 3 as immoral and "appeasing"—which I think we can agree doesn't follow the general debate principle of "think the best of your opponent" and does qualify as judgment and showing contempt. Of course, Stage 3 also tends to sneer at Stage 2. So we need pretty strict ground rules to have any hope in these conversations. Paul gives us these strict ground rules.

3. Make clear to yourself and others that you understand that your belief is not dogma and that reasonable, faithful people could disagree with you.

"So whatever you believe about these things keep between yourself and God."

This is tricky in all theological disputes that actually mean something to you. As I talk about above, we all do in fact believe whatever it is we believe.

It could have particularly unfortunate consequences in the dispute we're chatting about here regarding LGBT people and churches. I mean, is "keep this between yourself and God" code to LGBT people to stay in the closet, at least as far as churches are concerned? (To foreshadow: No.) Even trying to translate the issues Paul is describing to the dispute at hand—while I hope you'll grant that his issues were every bit as challenging to him as any of ours will be to us—could lead to unfortunate conclusions. Eating meat or celebrating the Sabbath are behaviors; the great bulk of my friends regard LGBT as an orientation.

Here's the value I see, even with all these challenges, from what Paul's pitching. Sincerely held religious disputes, as processed by fellow believers who are doing their best, require patience and perspective. History tells us that most disputable matters do, in fact, resolve within a reasonable period. While

Christians haven't settled the infant-versus-believer's baptism question and that one's been ongoing for millennia, issues like whether interracial marriage is okay took about twenty years to become so settled that people forgot it had ever been questioned.

4. **Do not exclude anyone from full participation in the community over disputable matters—so long as they also abide by these four principles.**

   "Therefore let us stop passing judgment on one another. Instead, make up your mind not to put any stumbling block or obstacle in the way of a brother or sister."

   Herein lies the rub. To talk more about this, let's take a look at Paul's loaded use of the terms "weak" and "strong." In what must have felt galling to most of the conservative Jews of his day, they were "the weak" in this analogy, because their consciences weren't "strong" enough to handle eating meat. The progressives—mostly Gentiles—were the "strong." Those who take the restrictive role in any religious dispute—women shouldn't preach to men; divorced and remarried people can't have full participation in the church; LGBT people can't lead and enjoy whatever privileges anyone else enjoys in the church—are the "weak" believers here.

   Paul's counsel is that the strong mustn't rub the weak's faces into their dispute. Meat-eaters shouldn't eat meat in front of the vegetarians. Conversely, the weak can't insist that the strong not eat meat in their own houses. "The one who does not eat everything must not judge the one who does, for God has accepted them. Who are you to judge someone else's servant?"

   In our current dispute about LGBT people, this means that, even during this time of dispute, LGBT people have full inclusion at all levels of our congregations—are treated in all respects like everyone else. They are not greeted with "welcome but," or told "we won't perform your wedding or you can't be a pastor." They are all-the-way welcome. In the spirit Paul is emphasizing in Romans 14, the LGBT person who is gifted and called to serve as a pastor is free to do so. Just as straight people in the church are free to marry, the LGBT person who wants to marry a person of the same gender is free to do so. LGBT people, again, are treated in all respects like everyone else. By the same token, more-conservative brothers and sisters don't need to change their convictions. They don't need to perform the wedding of a same-gender couple or do anything against their conscience *so long as* they entirely welcome and embrace those who feel differently, their LGBT friends very much included.

A central Blue Ocean leader has written an excellent book on this, as applied to the LGBT dispute, and has become a national leader on this approach which he calls "the Third Way."[78] You might wonder if, as applied to the LGBT dispute of the moment, this turns out not to be a Third Way at all, but to be the progressive way, often called "open and affirming." In practice, it does have things in common with "open and affirming," most notably in not excluding gay people from full participation in our churches at any level. But the "affirming" part of "open and affirming" seems to go against Paul's command here not to judge. To "affirm" someone, in this context, often means something like to "grant them moral approval." I have to meet them and ask myself, "As best as I can figure out, do I morally approve or disapprove of this person?" Then I decide, "I approve!" Along with Paul here, Jesus profoundly commands us not to judge anyone.[79] The issue in Third Way is not passing judgment positively or negatively on anyone, it's to include all people who hope to follow Jesus as the disputable matter works itself out.

---

78 Ken Wilson, *A Letter to My Congregation: An evangelical pastor's path to embracing people who are gay, lesbian and transgender into the company of Jesus* (David Crumm, 2014).

79 Matthew 7:1

"But what if I'm wrong?"

Paul is guiding us towards a Third Way that is neither
conservative nor liberal, at least in times of disputable matters.

I can assure you from a lot of examples that Paul's Third
Way doesn't work for people in the hard stages. They can't live
in the tension that the Third Way demands. They need to have
confidence that they're "right" even when times of genuine
dispute arise, and so they usually withdraw from Third Way
churches, often with cursing. Relationships are painfully
broken.

However, Paul's Third Way does, happily, work for people
in the soft stages, people who want Jesus more than they
want the form of a "correct religion." And let's be sympathetic
for a moment. Can you imagine the tension Paul was in
over eating meat sacrificed to idols? What if he was wrong?
On the terms of much of the Hebrew Bible, he'd be in huge,
massive, unbelievable sin! Sin so severe it could separate him
from any hope of heaven! How could he ask anyone to put
themselves into that kind of tension! No wonder Paul calls
the conservatives the "weak" ones! Aren't we *all* that kind
of "weak?" Which of us is willing to risk the consequences of
being wrong on matters so heatedly disputed?

And yet.

Is it worth mentioning that the possibility of being
wrong cuts both ways? Yes, you can be wrong by being too
permissive, but you can also be wrong by being too restrictive.
It seems entirely possible to me that, on Judgment Day, God
will wonder why we kept so many people away from the
Kingdom of Heaven. What gave us that right? Jesus even
weighs in directly on this side of the discussion. "Woe to you,
teachers of the law and Pharisees, you hypocrites! You shut the
door of the kingdom of heaven in people's faces."[80] The Third
Way emphasizes that, during times of heated disputes, we err
on the side of inclusion.

---

80 Matthew 23:13

The tension we embrace with the Third Way turns out to be at the heart of centered-set and of Stage 4. It forces us to trust in the God who speaks and guides. This centered-set God doesn't, in my experience, tell me that I'd better never hold the wrong views on disputed matters, or I'm going to be in big trouble. This actual, interactive God consistently encourages me to listen to him, read and enjoy the scriptures, talk to people I respect, go back to check in with him and to do my best. The God we're talking about here is, to review, only good. The pressure is not on us to be right. The pressure is on God to be powerful and loving.

Think of how this ties in with Stage 4. In Stage 2, as we look at the circle of truth that's about the same size that we are, what excuse do we have for not "standing on such clear truths?" In the vast circle of truth that we've entered into in Stage 4, we recognize that "truth" doesn't come at us from just one direction. It's consonant with the Bible and with people's actual experience (again "by their fruit" you'll know the truth[81]) and with the interactive God and with many more things. In the end, we trust that our good shepherd will *guide* us into all truth.[82]

With this in mind, the Third Way turns out to be central to Christian missions. Missionaries historically have often damaged native cultures by Westernizing very non-Western people in the name of "following Jesus." You can imagine the tensions for these missionaries! One commonly discussed example concerns polygamous cultures. Western missionaries, for reasons you might guess, commonly commanded polygamous converts to choose one of their wives, to embrace monogamy. The consequence of that was devastating—the rejected women and their children were cast off from their families and thrown into poverty and, for the women, often into prostitution. It had society-wide, horrible repercussions.

---

81 Matthew 7:16-20

82 John 16:13. "But when he, the Spirit of truth, comes, he will guide you into all the truth."

And yet, to the missionaries in question, the Bible was clear! When the Bible appears "clear" even as a given interpretation causes fruit that is clearly bad, we've entered into disputable matters territory, but moving forward takes real confidence in a living, speaking God. It's not possible to take such a risk with a distant God who will condemn the poor missionary who "gets it wrong" on such a consequential thing. Those missionaries have only one, destructive option.

The Third Way allows us to recognize fellow lovers of Jesus who didn't grow up in our culture, who come to the table with different assumptions. It allows us mutually to learn from one another. It seems to me that the lack of a Third Way is a key reason that churchgoing collapsed throughout Europe, the onetime seat of Christian faith. European countries in that era were largely monocultural. Swedes lived in Sweden, Italians in Italy. In each case, when monocultural Christianity came under attack in a given country, there were no countervailing, faithful voices to offer a different perspective, and so the house fell. Ecclesiastes teaches us that "a cord of three strands is not quickly broken," but we're doomed if we're alone.[83] In a nice bonus, the Third Way allows us to learn from faithful people in other cultures without asking us to violate our own consciences! That's quite a gift.

It's not a cure-all. It is crucial.

Disagreeing over consequential things is just flat out hard. Religious disagreements can strain and sometimes end relationships. The Third Way doesn't avoid that pain.

But, as Paul knew it would, it does provide a way forward for the gospel to thrive in a changing time. It teaches us a new way to rely on a living, speaking, loving God who is calling the whole world to himself.

---

83 Ecclesiastes 4:12

6

Let's Defuse Religion's Seeds of Its Own Destruction

Religion will be the thing that blows us all up, or it will be the antidote to the thing that could blow us all up.

AFTER THE 2015 ISIS attacks on Paris, it was hard to avoid punditry that Made Sense of It All. The conservative columns I read tied the attacks to a failure of everything Democratic, from gun control to immigration reform to a weakling in the Oval Office who, among other things, wouldn't call out the evils of Islam. The liberal writers pointed out that many Muslims clearly denounced ISIS and that the attacks reflected radicalism rather than Islam en toto and that we should feel bad for ignoring other ISIS attacks just that week in Beirut (and Turkey and Baghdad) while we only highlighted attacks on white Westerners. Everyone was responding to a world that felt less safe than it did before the attacks.

David Brooks, in *The New York Times,* used the moment to promote a book by Rabbi Jonathan Sacks called *Not in God's Name: Confronting Religious Violence.* He said that Sacks debunked the thought that the upcoming century will be one of increasing secularization.[84]

---

84 http://www.nytimes.com/2015/11/17/opinion/finding-peace-within-the-holy-texts.html

Secular people have always had fewer children than religious people and so always find themselves swamped under by swelling religion. But Brooks told us that "Sacks emphasizes that it is not religion itself that causes violence. In their book *Encyclopedia of Wars*, Charles Phillips and Alan Axelrod surveyed 1,800 conflicts and found that less than 10 percent had any religious component at all." What religion promoted in these wars wasn't itself—it was "groupishness," the certainty that your group was all good and the opponent was all evil. More Brooks: "This leads to acts of what Sacks calls altruistic evil, or acts of terror in which the self-sacrifice involved somehow is thought to confer the right to be merciless and unfathomably cruel."

I've experienced, first-hand, religion that reinforces this groupishness and other religion that pushes against it. Have you? Let's say we concede that groupishness as described here is a bad thing, I wonder if you would feel queasy about entirely leaving it behind. A good deal of the pastors I've listened to over the years would have strong cautions. Is the alternative to groupishness something we might call … compromise? Or relativism? I mean—these pastors might say—of course we don't want to be monsters like the terrorists in Paris and elsewhere, but unlike them we're *not* monsters and do we really want to suggest that God can helpfully be found outside of our group? If we concede that, have we betrayed Jesus,[85] who is Truth in human form?

---

85 Scriptures that would quickly come up would be John 14:6 ("I am the way, and the truth, and the life. No one comes to the Father except through me") or Luke 9:26 ("Whoever is ashamed of me and my words, the Son of Man will be ashamed of them when he comes in his glory and in the glory of the Father and of the holy angels") or any number of great passages that tell us to stay away from error (just one for our purposes here: Isaiah 32:6—"For fools speak folly, their hearts are bent on evil: They practice ungodliness and spread error concerning the Lord") or 2 Timothy 4:3 ("For the time will come when people will not put up with sound doctrine. Instead, to suit their own desires, they

Don't label me.

Those of us in the church trade often chafe in the face of a very reasonable question from someone checking out our church: What kind of church are we? Evangelical? Liberal? Pentecostal? Liturgical? What?

I can dodge the question for myself if I want to—I grew up atheist. Still, I led a church in an evangelical group of churches, and I can attest that almost all of my pastor friends wrestled with that label. For one thing, the meaning of the word "evangelical" was no longer controlled by churches that used it—it was now a cultural label that, in the press, pretty much meant "conservative-Christian-right-wing-anti-gay-anti-intellectual." To the outside world, evangelicals were the people who supported the most extreme Republican candidates, the candidates that had to drop out after the first few primaries. No matter how much my friends and I might be tempted to reclaim to us what to us seemed like a "more pure" meaning of the word ("Evangelical" just means "Bible-person." The "evangel" is literally "the good news of the Bible!" All that other stuff is not at the heart of it. Evangelicals look to the Bible to guide them towards loving God and loving their neighbors. Evangelicals were at the heart of the abolitionist movement for Pete's sake! Ever hear of William Wilberforce? And "anti-intellectual?!" What about C.S. Lewis?![86] Tim Keller?! These are smart people!), that horse seemed to be out of the barn.

Whatever the chafing, though, churches do need to decide both how to market themselves and what other churches

---

will gather around them a great number of teachers to say what their itching ears want to hear") or … I'll stop. It's a defined way of looking at the world!

86 Yes, absolutely, I'm with you—C.S. Lewis was not an evangelical! He was Anglican! The man smoked like a chimney and liked his alcohol! He never attended an evangelical church in his life! But try telling that to most of my evangelical friends.

they're going to hang out with. Other traditions might well have good things to offer—and my evangelical pastor friends do occasionally read books from those other streams—but we do need to swap resources with church friends and, I mean, it's good to know who "our people" are.

Labels are really helpful, and they're profoundly unhelpful.

Labels are reductionist. Think about your own religious label. Does it define what you believe? Or are you a more complex person than that label suggests?

Let's think about the most basic label among Protestants. Are you "conservative" or are you "liberal" (or the preferred related label, "progressive")? Interestingly, even those most primary labels are quite new categories. Jesus, Paul, Augustine, Luther and Theresa of Avila would not have known what to do with them. Those labels showed up in the late 19th century when educated people were saying that truth was defined by the scientific method. They increasingly saw religious people as gullible and stupid. Religious people believed in virgin births, people being swallowed by big fish (and living to tell the tale) and the sun stopping its rotation around the earth at helpful times. In response to this disdain, some religious people adopted a scientific-method-like religious term, "fundamentalist." This new term for a person was for someone who looked to the "fundamentals," to the atoms of truth that you couldn't split. To these people, the unsplittable atom was the Bible—Truth itself! Churches with "Bible" in the title started to pop up. Fundamentalists emphasized Bible teaching even over, say, the work of a living God, which could seem subjective (the thing modernists mocked[87]). On the other side of the spectrum, newfound "liberal" churches conceded the point that, sure, the miracles in the Bible were a little embarrassing, but it was unassailable that Jesus was the

---

87 "Objective truth"—now there's a good modernist idea that no one before 1650 would have known what to do with.

epitome of a good citizen. His ethics certainly were worth our emulating over anyone else's.

Both of these choices are what we've called bounded-set. Conservative churches focus on the boundaries, on what separates them from the godless people outside, and so preachers spend a lot of time looking at what is or isn't personal sin. Is porn-viewing sin? Drinking alcohol? Going to an R-rated movie? Believing the wrong thing about a current hot-button topic? Liberal churches do the same thing—preachers focus on societal sins, on not loving the poor and weak, on problems like racism, sexism or ageism. These two bounded-sets fight with each other over which sins are really sins. What can get lost in either conservative or liberal churches is centered-set, helping each other turn our arrows towards the living Jesus who then will give us living feedback, living connection, living help and living relationship.

On a related note, my Blue Ocean pastor friends seem to have abandoned any interest in reclaiming a word like, say, "evangelical." Yes, it's a bounded-set word, but even trying to reclaim it for our allegedly-higher purpose focuses us on how we fit in with this one group of religious people as being "our people." Most of my Blue Ocean pastor friends seem to be finding a different group of people who feel like "their people"—quite a large group of people called "all people." A bounded-set label doesn't help connect us to that group.

Just for a moment, I'll assume you're sympathetic to this perspective. You don't even particularly feel conservative or liberal—at least as the thing which best defines your perspective. Sermons which focus on who are good people and who are bad people—from either perspective—seem limiting to you. You'd rather focus on how to connect with God or others, than on whom to separate from. Here's the dilemma. Without a label, are you ... anything? Words can actually be helpful.[88]

---

88 Here's a related story. Some years back, I'd seen several hundred previously secular people experience faith in Jesus as a part of a class

Labels in the church world also tell us where to hunt for particular repositories of wisdom. So, if you're willing to wander a little beyond your own group, maybe you learn from the social justice people how to think about a church's place in the wider society. Maybe you learn from the renewalist people about how to experience the Holy Spirit. You learn from the liturgical people about how to pray when you don't know what to pray. You learn from the evangelicals about how to have a personal relationship with Jesus.[89]

Let's try thinking about it as a swirl.

We previously quoted the late Phyllis Tickle about solus Jesus. Here's another idea she proposes.[90]

Imagine a page in which those four labels—"social justice," "renewalist," "liturgical" and "evangelical" each occupy a quadrant. Situate which of these traditions would be your starting point. Now imagine following a swirl through the other quadrants, then back through your starting-point quadrant, all the time moving closer and closer to the center.

I helped develop, called Seek. The church I was leading was called "Vineyard Christian Fellowship of Greater Boston"—a long name and one that, I wondered, might be a little bounded-set. (Since I've left, it has a new name: "Reservoir Church.") Were these secular people who'd come to Jesus happy that we used even the broad category of "Christian" or would it have been easier if we had a different name? We got a couple hundred survey responses from these folks, and the response entirely went one way. They liked "Christian." They liked that we called the thing we did on Sunday mornings "church." Why? Because these labels made them feel safe, even if they were secular and just checking the church out. Those words seemed straightforward to them.

89 And a whole lot more, in each of those cases! Even those quick compliments are reductive.

90 As before, this is from her mega-influential late-period book *The Great Emergence: How Christianity is Changing and Why* (Baker, 2008).

In this swirl, we're encouraged to take a tour through the wisdom embodied by the other historic, Christian traditions to the point that we'll increasingly embody all four in large measure. Most of us will by no means lose our starting point, which is the tradition we grew up with or which connects best to us. Nonetheless, in this swirl we become "ecumenical" in that we recognize that each of the great Christian traditions has something important to offer us and we're as proactive as we can be in learning what that is.

This does a few good things for us.

1. It prods spiritual growth.

You'll remember our look at the spirituality of childlike dependence on a living God. This God speaks to us and leads us and, as a good shepherd, can be trusted to guide us through great times and times of real suffering. This connected, adventurous journey of faith is at the heart of what we understand spiritual growth to be.

This swirl can help us on that journey.

Poking our head into these different repositories of wisdom jolts us into understanding the richness of life with Jesus in a way we can't access if we stay camped out in our starting point.

2. It breaks us out of groupishness.

In centered-set, we're hoping to connect with the living God and to encourage and learn from others trying to do the same. Yet, we all naturally gravitate towards groups. We're social creatures! When I root for the Red Sox and against the Yankees, I can imagine a given Yankees fan who's a lovely person and whom I'd very much enjoy getting to know.

But, in my groupish self, I actually can't imagine that, because that lovely Yankees fan doesn't exist as an individual, only as part of a hated group.

Being ecumenical (the mildly-archaic noun form of the word is "ecumenism"[91]) in practice, not just in attitude, helps

---

91 This was a thing in the Christian world 70 or so years ago. The World Council of Churches was founded in 1948 to encourage

break down this groupishness, and—if David Brooks and
Rabbi Sacks are right—that's a very, very, very important thing
in a volatile world. It goes back to the centered-set insight
that perhaps we're not all just one "arrow," which is either
turned towards or away from Jesus. We're actually more like
a hundred arrows, any one of which every person we ever
meet can help turn towards Jesus. It goes back to the Third
Way insight that, with just a few ground rules in place, we can
and should learn about Jesus from very different people than
we find in "our group." Ecumenism among Christians starts,
understandably, with the great Christian traditions that have
each thrived over millennia. With that as a base, it permits
learning from all people, all in service towards learning more
about following Jesus.

3. It opens the door to diversity.

You've figured out by now in this list that I'm just finding
different ways to make the same point, but this phrasing does
offer a shade of difference. We've recently learned a lot more
about how churches interact with ethnic and socioeconomic
diversity.[92]

Namely, they almost always reinforce homogeneity.
Because churches offer such unique opportunities for intimacy
and friendship, they profoundly sift out who is and isn't "like

---

ecumenism. Famous leaders like Reinhold Niebuhr and Dietrich
Bonhoeffer pushed for this. Vatican II (1962-1965) nudged the
Catholic Church this direction. Evangelicalism has often operated as
a protest against ecumenism (the National Association of Evangelicals
was founded in 1943 as a protest against an earlier ecumenical group,
and anticipated what was soon to come with the World Council of
Churches).

92 Great places to start in this would be early books in the field like
Michael Emerson and Christian Smith's *Divided by Faith: Evangelical
Religion and the Problem of Race in America* (Oxford, 2001) or George
Yancey's *One Body One Spirit: Principles of Successful Multiracial
Churches* (IVP, 2003).

us." We feel most at home among people with similar life backgrounds.

Increasingly, younger churchgoers are pushing for diverse congregations. Once they leave home, colleges and workplaces are diverse in ways that the suburbs or neighborhoods they grew up in weren't. Diversity, learning to work and befriend and follow Jesus together, becomes important to them. Ecumenism teaches some of these key skills.

4. It treats us like adults.

In our groupishness, insight that comes from other groups is suspect. In its most-extreme form, we get the message that there's only a limited set of insights that are safe to learn. Ecumenism tells us that others have insights about following Jesus that we can learn from. Pastors in these traditions aren't parent figures keeping young children safe from corruption. They trust that, as they encourage congregants to turn their arrows towards Jesus and get the wonderful feedback Jesus gives them as a result, these congregants can be trusted to find further encouragement towards turning towards Jesus wherever that encouragement can be found. The God of these pastors isn't eager to condemn us if, in our sincere desire to turn our arrows towards Jesus, we get some item of doctrine "wrong." This God is about actual, experienced connection, not abstract "rightness." He's centered-set. A congregant from an evangelical congregation might well find a good deal of liturgical wisdom to be dull or off-topic, as might be true in reverse. However, this congregant will be keeping their eyes open for how God is speaking to them from this new quadrant. In the Stage 4 big-circle, little-us world, we recognize that there's a lot we don't yet know about God.

Jesus is excited about this.

Again, a center-point of Jesus' mission on earth was to "break dividing walls" between people[93], to blast through groupishness. When Jesus' disciples run into related but

93 Ephesians 2:14

differing groups, they get groupish—they want to call down
fire from heaven to burn those people up.[94] But Jesus teaches
"whoever is not against us is for us."[95]

Let's revisit our earlier question. For all these benefits, does
this sort of ecumenism qualify as a "compromise" of our faith?

Again, if we live in a bounded set, "compromise" is finding
wisdom outside of our set. By definition, what's outside is
beyond the boundary of sin, and so it can only corrupt us.

In centered-set, all we're looking to find is anything that
helps us direct ourselves towards the living, interactive Jesus.
Any wisdom that does this is much appreciated. Certainly,
we might find ourselves intrigued by perspectives that we
realize are dampening our connection to Jesus, and to the
abundance he promises. In this case we're most certainly
advised to repent, to "turn again" to the things that bring us
life in God. We'll discover that experientially. As a category,
"religion"—which we might loosely define as "looking for rules
to determine if we or others are good or bad people"—does
get characterized as the kind of false lead that will hurt our
connection to Jesus.[96] It's another word for groupishness. We'll
want to avoid this as we swirl through the quadrants, each of
which will have their own form of it. But we're keeping our
eyes quite wide open for fresh, connecting insights.

Are there, then, any words we can use to describe this faith?
If firm labels limit us, are any descriptions safe to use?

I don't know. I tend to like descriptions rather than labels:
"I'm trying to follow Jesus" rather than "I'm a [whatever

---

94 Luke 9:54

95 Mark 9:40. In Matthew 12:30, Jesus also teaches the inverse—
"whoever is not for me is against me"—in which he's seeming to talk
about spiritual opposition. So it seems there are ways in which we can
assume good will, while at the same time recognizing that we're also
looking for partners in Jesus' mission.

96 1 Corinthians 4:3 ("I care very little if I am judged by you or by any
human court; indeed, I do not even judge myself.") is a particularly
intriguing case study along these lines.

category] Christian."[97] I also find myself wanting to take note of my audience. In some cases, "I'm a Christian" might be just the right answer to a question. And so I am! Biographical approaches to the question also seem fair enough to me. "I pastored a church in an evangelical group of churches" is flat-true in my case. "I grew up atheist, but had a powerful encounter with Jesus" would also be true in my case.

The heart of the insight in this fifth Blue Ocean distinctive focuses not so much on how we label ourselves, as it is focused on our heart to learn from all traditions of people trying to follow Jesus, to grow together as we, with Jesus, break rather than reinforce dividing walls.

Will we be groupish? Or will we be the antidote to groupishness?

Our answer has high stakes.

---

97 One evangelical church movement, feeling that even the word "Christian" had taken on bad popular connotations, encouraged replacing "I'm a Christian" with "I'm a Christ-follower." That struck me as weird jargon, though clearly when we phrased it as a process ("I'm trying to follow Jesus") rather than as a noun, it worked great for me. Proving that we each need to find our way here.

7

Engaging the Secular World Turns Out to be Super Fun

Imagine two circles.

A FEW YEARS back, I got together with a businessman named Rich. He'd earlier said to me, "Dave, I've been in churches my whole life and what I see from you and your friends feels different in a good way. If there's ever anything I can do for you in my business capacity, I'd take it as a favor if you'd ask me."

I asked him. My book, *Not the Religious Type*, was going to come out in about a month. I realized I wasn't entirely clear about what I was hoping for from it. I actually hadn't ever pitched it to publishers. Instead, a senior editor at a publishing house had heard me speak at a joint Christian/atheist event and came up afterwards to pitch me writing a book.

I wasn't even hoping to ask Rich's help in marketing it—I didn't know much about publishing, but I assumed that promotional help would have had to have happened earlier in the process. Instead, I wanted his help in thinking through the bigger picture. Did this book teach us anything about a worthy, Jesus-focused mission in the larger world?

Okay, Rich said. Who was I writing the book for?

I drew a circle in the air and said, "Let's say this represents the churchgoing world." Then, I drew a circle that bumped up against it and said, "And let's say this represents the secular world. It's not that those are the only two circles in the world—there are other religious traditions and I'm sure lots of other circles besides, but let's just look at these two. I'd say I wrote the book to the line between them. There's a swath that spills over to the churchgoing world—churchgoers who may be contented religiously, but who nonetheless identify mostly with the secular world, and feel alone in that among their churchgoing friends. There's also another swath that covers secular people who feel as if there might really be Something Going On Out There."

Rich liked that answer and said that it explained what he was driving at in his affirming comments earlier. "So," he said, "let's find out if there's a market for this perspective." He had a friend who was a booker with the (dearly mourned) Colbert Report. Why not just get me on the show?

That, I said, seemed ridiculous. Why would they want a nobody like me?

Rich countered that this was important stuff, this "line" we were talking about. Maybe it wasn't just the line between churchgoing and secular people, maybe it was the line between, say, red and blue states, which appeared to be pulling apart from one another at a dizzying rate. Maybe speaking to folks in a swath around this line was the single most important thing for America's future!

He called his friend. The man took Rich seriously, kicked it upstairs, and got back to Rich in a couple of days. He said that both Rich and I were right. I was right that I was a nobody and they didn't want me, but Rich was right that speaking about that line was, in their estimation, as important a task as there was today. Without someone—or many someones—speaking helpfully in exactly that way, we were headed to a kind of fragmentation worse than we'd yet seen as a country. So, he encouraged Rich—the moment Dave is a somebody, get right in touch with us and we'll be good to go.

This is the last of the Blue Ocean distinctives.

Here's one last review.

1. Our primary framework is SOLUS JESUS.

2. Our primary metaphor is CENTERED-SET.

3. Our approach to spiritual development is CHILDLIKE FAITH.

4. Our approach to controversial issues is THIRD WAY.

5. Our approach to other churches is ECUMENICAL.

6. Our approach to secular culture is JOYFUL ENGAGEMENT.

Consider two types of revival.

Let's think about the man's point from a religious perspective. I'm a revivalist at heart. It's what convinced both Grace and me that we should get married; we were the only people we knew who regularly prayed that God would let us participate in a revival before we died.[98] We've each read quite a bit about revivals. She convinced me to overlook the dated prose, and to get all the amazing stuff about the 1920s Welsh Revival from an old book called *Rees Howells: Intercessor*. I gave her interesting facts about the Great Awakenings. We both then ended up in a group of churches that emerged out of what may be America's last revival, the Jesus Movement of the early 1970s.

After all that study, it appears that there are two kinds of revivals. Both are real, but yield very different, long-range outcomes. One of the two would, I think, encourage the

---

98 As time has gone on, I know less and less what a religious revival actually is. How would we know if one hit? As we've talked about here, so much of any religion boils down to culture, so whenever any religious culture expands its turf, to them God's revival has come! However, I remain a revivalist nonetheless, even as I acknowledge that this is a pretty primary problem. I pray for things like "a centered-set revival."

Colbert Report booker. The other would discourage him. One revival, perhaps, is the cause of many of America's problems, and the other is the solution.

America was shaped by holiness revivals.

One you might call a holiness revival. The Great Awakenings, tent revivals and the Welsh Revival each fit this profile. A central idea of a holiness revival is that, if churchgoers start paying serious attention to their own holiness—if they become more godly and dedicated—revival will break out from them to the rest of the world. I have friends praying in exactly this way with groups in California and Missouri. Perhaps the central verse for this approach is an obscure one from 2 Chronicles: "Then if my people who are called by my name will humble themselves and pray and seek my face and turn from their wicked ways, I will hear from heaven and will forgive their sins and restore their land."[99]

Think about Jonathan Edwards. He was a deep thinker and yet it's the non-scholarly "Sinners in the Hands of an Angry God" that defines his legacy. Repentance by believers, to him, is the start of repentance by the world. The Welsh Revival talked about closing down saloons and jails. It all boils down to holiness.

In praise of holiness revivals.

These revivals were incredible. *A lot* of people converted. They had social impact.

And I have a long history of loving them. I kid you not: as a college graduation gift, one friend got me the complete, encyclopedia-length works of Jonathan Edwards, knowing I would read them. Finney, Whitefield, Wesley, Moody, the tent revivalists and the Jesus Movement leaders, along with Rees Howells, have all given me tremendous inspiration. I love the fervency of these revivals. I often wonder why, like these old-time revivalists, I seem to care so much about something as

---

99 7:14

distant and abstract as participating in a big move of God. Why can't I just go about my business like everybody else? My best answer is that massive revivals represent a unique kind of hope, a hope that for, however brief a time, we can be a part of something so good, so connected to God, so meaningful, so breaking-down-of-barriers, so imbued with a divine energy that we by no means created. It's the hope of being swept up in something. The occasional, widely-inspiring political campaign strikes me as a flickering shadow of this sort of hope. I wonder if maybe everyone hopes for this if we just look hard enough.

But there were downsides.

The incredible, fervent holiness revivals did bring real downsides.

For one, they tended to be short-lived. Most traces of the Welsh Revival were gone within twenty years. The jails and bars were back in business. Upstate New York and New England, the center of the Great Awakenings, are now the most secular parts of America. One hypothesis is that they became "burned-over districts." So many traveling revivalists preached hellfire in such a short period of time that they left behind trauma that's continued for generations.

Some of our biggest problems have their roots here. If, say, the holiness-revival world is divided into "serious Christians" and the reprobate (damned)—if it's bounded-set to the extreme—then there's not much incentive for working together. So, we have our politics today, in which the parties— particularly the party most known for being religious—speak in saved-versus-reprobate terms. Why would you compromise by working alongside the devil?

There were, of course, absolutely some positive social consequences from these Awakenings, not least the abolitionist movement (which, granted, was opposed by religious Americans as well). But perhaps the most noteworthy social fruit of the Awakenings was Prohibition, in which the establishment religious Americans (English Puritans) drew moral lines against more recent religious immigrants from Ireland and Italy, Catholic countries that had drinking cultures. One religious culture condemned another religious culture.

The Franciscan Revival looked quite different.

Let's contrast this to a different type of revival, one with different roots, a different call to action, and very different, long-range consequences.[100]

Where holiness revivals focus on boundaries—who's inside or outside of holy living—the Franciscan Revival focused on a center: the beautiful, joy-engendering Jesus.

Holiness revivals are a profound "no"—to sin, if nothing else. The Franciscan Revival is a profound "yes"—to Jesus and joy and the fullness of life.

So Francis was a young, wealthy man whose dreams of worldly glory—being a famous knight—fell apart. In his dismay, he had a vision of Jesus that led him to take radical steps like renouncing his wealth. Responding to a vision to "rebuild my church," he started by rebuilding a local, dilapidated church. Then, others joined him both because of his infectiously joyful spirit, and his simple vision of hearing and obeying the delightful Jesus.

They began to travel from town to town as Jesus' "troubadours," singing and preaching about Jesus' love and power. The revival that followed was markedly different than the holiness revivals.

That said, it's not that these revivals were completely at odds. Francis had a strong personal code of holiness. Famously, when he was sexually tempted, he would roll naked in snow or bramble bushes in order to "discipline" his body. As we've

---

100 I'm about to pitch a sweeping theory. I, of course, buy my own theory. I've gotten feedback from historians, including a Franciscan, who offered their caveats. All to say that, by nature, sweeping historical theories invite pushback and quibbling, so be warned.

noted, the Awakenings and the Welsh Revival offered many people a strong encounter with Jesus. But they led with very different messages.

A virtuous cycle between the Christian and secular worlds.

The Franciscan Revival—which focused on connecting with the goodness and presence of Jesus, rather than on a call to a "more serious Christian living"—had a remarkable effect as a new wave of enthusiasm for Jesus swept first across Italy and then across Europe. It lasted for three hundred years.

It also catalyzed a remarkable interplay with the larger culture.[101] Rather than driving a wedge between "serious" religious insiders and everyone else, each side spurred the other onto huge, mutually-beneficial leaps forward. While the Italian Renaissance had begun to show itself by the time Francis started his ministry, the wholesale change in Italian culture produced by Francis's revival was, to G.K. Chesterton and other thinkers, at the heart of what became the Renaissance. The groupthink of the religious middle ages was replaced by a heartfelt sense that you personally could connect to God, and to truth and innovation. Without the changes Francis and his followers brought, we would say goodbye to the Renaissance's leaps forward in government, art, education, science, philosophy and other disciplines.

Then the larger society returned the favor.

Without the Renaissance, there wouldn't have been a Reformation, which exploded the gospel from being almost exclusively a regional, European endeavor to one that went

---

101 G.K. Chesterton's *St. Francis of Assisi* takes a vivid, uniquely-G.K.-Chesterton look at this interplay. It's worth noting that the idea of a "secular" culture in that era would have been nonsensical. You were born into a religion, but there was very much a developing story of a "larger" culture, as Chesterton documents, that was also a "secular" culture before this timeline was done.

worldwide.[102] Luther, Calvin and Zwingli were steeped in Renaissance thinking. This gave them the perspective to critique the existing religious order, and to offer such a compelling new vision.

Then the Reformation birthed the Enlightenment, which itself birthed modern science and the entire modern world.

The scientific method wasn't thinkable in a world that honored tradition to the extent that the medieval world did. Galileo hadn't been imprisoned and tortured because of his scientific observations, but because of his challenge to "what the church had always taught." Luther and the rest of the reformers won the day that the individual could have their own encounter with truth. Hello Enlightenment!

To recap, one type of revival, focused on the need for religious people to become more seriously religious, for all its benefits often splits off the religious and secular worlds to the point that they can only demonize each other. This then drives their world into stagnation and animosity.

But, the other does just the reverse and offers Jesus to all people, which catalyzes a profound, virtuous cycle. The good stuff that the first produces is short-lived, and has lasting, negative consequences. The other kicks off a positive and generative cycle for all people for centuries.[103]

---

102 There were certainly some non-European churches before this! But the Reformation empowered what's often called the modern missionary movement.

103 Like all movements, the Franciscans hit some speedbumps after their founder died. However, what I find encouraging is that, by that point, the "horse" of this virtuous cycle was out of the barn. It no longer required their leadership.

Here's an intriguing picture from Jesus that drove Francis' vision.

> *Just as Moses lifted up the snake in the wilderness,*
> *so the Son of Man must be lifted up, that everyone*
> *who believes may have eternal life in him. ... And*
> *I, when I am lifted up from the earth, will draw all*
> *people to myself. (John 3:14-15, 12:32)*

We've already touched on this last verse, but let's think about this in a little more depth. This is an obscure reference. Jesus is calling to mind an incident in the Exodus. The Israelites were angering God with their incessant complaining, so he sent poisonous snakes into their camp. They went to Moses to see if he could address their sudden crisis. Moses asked God, who told him that, if he created a bronze image of a snake, stuck it on a stick, and held the stick up, anyone who looked that direction wouldn't die from the poison.

Jesus is foreshadowing the cross, when he would, in fact, be lifted up on a stick. But the innovation comes a few chapters later in John's gospel—if *we* lift him up like the snake on the stick, *he* promises to draw all people to himself.

Francis realized that our job, then, was to "lift Jesus up, like the snake on the stick"—and that, having done that, we're done. Jesus promises to take it from there. Francis understood that our temptation will be to whap people over the head with the stick in case they missed what was going on. The religious leadership of his day majored on behavioral commandments for the laity, on shaping a "godly society." They drew swords against "the infidels" in the Crusades. Francis, instead, famously went to Malik-al-Kamil, the sultan of Egypt and a prominent Muslim general. Francis expected to be martyred, but he was determined not to draw swords against the sultan, but to offer Jesus to him and see what Jesus would do. After some tense moments, not only was Francis not martyred, the sultan became an ally and gave Francis the land in Jerusalem that became the first Franciscan monastery.

Francis majored not on behavior change, but on this lifting-up of Jesus, a fundamentally different, centered-set act, and one that took almost a generation for the religious establishment of his day to understand. Then Jesus drew much of Europe to himself, which led to blessing building upon blessing—for everyone—for centuries.

Getting back to my conversation with Rich.

Let's think back to the bullet points from my conversation with Rich.

- Two circles: one representing churchgoers, the other representing the secular world.
- "Speaking to the line" in a way which could provide an overlapping, mutually beneficial conversation that might benefit both circles.

The Holiness Revival model, clearly, couldn't, in good conscience, take on that project. That sort of "compromise" could never get the job done.

The Franciscan model, though, has a lot of possibilities in this regard.

This provokes some unlearning from people of good will on both sides. We run annual Blue Ocean Summits which draw churchgoers from many different states. One year, our two keynote speakers were secular—one a bestselling novelist, the other a Harvard-trained psychiatrist. The novelist, who'd a few years ago made contact with these ideas and liked them, said a quick yes to coming … but then dropped all communication for months before finally agreeing to come only four days in advance. He apologized, but said he was terrified to go into a church after very bad childhood experiences. Many good-hearted secular people are skeptical that something like "speaking to the line" is possible.

On the churchgoing side, some Blue Ocean enthusiasts have big dreams and excitedly talk about things like having gatherings along these lines in every zip code in America (and beyond), and about attracting the most talented faith leaders into this Franciscan endeavor.

The faith leaders who've become most committed to this have discovered a new humility. Having initially responded enthusiastically, they've realized that sustaining this for a lifetime will require new skills and new partnerships. So they've gathered in cohorts, studied together, and swapped stories and ideas. These people are making feature films, short films, writing novels and starting websites.

The early returns are heartening, on both sides of the line. I spoke at an MIT event with a pastor-turned-atheist of some prominence and a packed house of students. Our (secular) host, by the time the electric event was over, asked if this could become an annual tradition. On the religious side, the average church that finds their way into the Blue Ocean conversation reports a 40% increase in non-churchgoing people who join them within the first year. It's all pretty fun.

Looking inward. Or looking at Jesus.

In the holiness revivals, to a great extent we're looking at ourselves. We're taking stock. Are we serious about holiness? Are we serious about prayer? Are we, well, *serious*?

But Francis looked at Jesus rather than at himself and was flooded with joy. This joy freed him to notice the world around him. He delighted in birds, animals, flowers, the stars, the sun, the moon and he preached to them. One doesn't picture Jonathan Edwards paying a lot of attention to the birds. Centered-set, in Francis's vision, grounds us in our actual world. Bounded-set abstracts us from the world into an ideal of holy behavior. Centered-set—looking at and drinking in life from Jesus—intrinsically leads to joy. This becomes both our offer to others around us (who doesn't want joy?) and our fuel to walk into a great, terrifying, mysterious journey into the heart of the wild and vast larger world.

A few experiences have helped teach me this lesson.

Our church has prayed quite a bit for our city, and we loved the vision of a national leader who convenes large, city-wide prayer gatherings. So, we connected with him, financially supported his people's mega prayer gathering in our city and helped them start a local prayer center. However, we hit a bump when I read a letter to their financial supporters saying that the reason they were setting up a prayer center in Cambridge was to pray against the evil influence of Harvard—which they wrote was the primary font that spewed secular demonism into the world.

I called the leader.

Listen, I said, I'm so glad for all the prayer you all are planning to offer the city I love. But could I suggest just one changed word in your mission statement? Rather than praying "against" Harvard, could you pray "for" Harvard? For all I know, you're totally right in your harsh assessment of Harvard. But if they're somehow spewing evil into the world, I'm confident—knowing a lot of professors and deans and administrators there, many of whom came to our church—that that's not what they're trying to do. Harvard devotes considerable resources to trying to address some of the worst problems on earth. They're staffed by people, churchgoing and non-churchgoing, who are quite earnestly trying to help the world at pretty great, unequalled levels. So, if you're worried that they're not doing that as your type of Christians, by all means pray for their enlightenment and conversion! Awesome! Whether or not we agree with your assessment of what Harvard does as an institution, we could certainly get behind your prayers that they'd see the light. And those dedicated people could use intercessors, to be sure! And that, it seems to me, would still entirely fit the mandate you're appealing to in your letters to your donors. Either way, you've come to a strategic place to pray for God's work there. Seems like a win!

But no. The leader said that his charge was to curse Harvard, not bless it. If I was praying "for" such godless people, it meant I was one of them and he and I wouldn't be speaking to each other anymore. We haven't since.

I also think of the secular, middle-aged woman who ran a very prominent literary group.

I pitched her about a literary project that would "write to the line" that Rich and I talked about in service of offering (soft Stage 2 and soft Stage 3) religious and nonreligious Americans a place to connect. She was entirely intrigued. "But," she said, "those religious people worry me. They're trying to take over the country. We nonreligious people are under constant assault by them." You know, I said, did she realize that the religious people I talked to felt very much the same about her and her friends—that they were the ones trying to take over the country? "But how could they possibly feel that way?" she asked in open-hearted befuddlement. "My friends and I are such nice people!"

Or I think about an epiphany I had on a soccer field.

Belmont, Massachusetts—my home at the time—has an astounding soccer program for young kids. Every year, hundreds of kids participate in "Second Soccer," a parent-run program to introduce soccer and provide healthy Saturday morning activity for pretty much every young child in town. Three of my kids participated when they were the right age, all very positively. One day I was the parent who took my daughter there. I was dazzled. On this massive field were about two dozen game fields. If I looked up from seeing my young daughter's team play, I'd see a massive swath of humanity. Not to mention the parents there were so nice. My daughter, for instance, wasn't motivated by soccer. Her game plan was to hang back from the action and talk to her friends as they trailed behind the ball. Her coach, though, was great— so encouraging to her and the other kids, so sacrificial in his time and money, just a gift. I realized several things in a burst. (A) These parents were all nicer people than I was. There was no way I was willing to coach their kids. I was too busy and protective of my time. (B) Statistically, maybe 5% of these parents and children were churchgoers. (C) Proving my bounded-set roots, I found myself asking: So … if things don't change on the churchgoing front for them … are 95% of these people who are all nicer than I am going to hell?

I simultaneously had two thoughts race through me, one a flow of religious arguments and the other, I think, that was the actual Jesus trying to get my attention.

Some of the religious arguments that raced through my mind were: Heaven has nothing to do with how *nice* they are— it's only about Jesus! (That was unsatisfying, seeming both super-heady and mean.) Or: Dave, you call these people "nice" because of this one snippet of life with them on the soccer field, but they're strangers to you, so you have no idea in the big picture if they're nice or not. For all you know, a given dad or mom could be nice in this moment and the worst sort of abuser at home or at the office. (Now we were deep into head games. Was I allowed to experience these people's good qualities in the moment, or was that off-limits?)

But the other voice had a whole different, much cheerier and less grimly-resolute feel. "Dave," this voice was saying, "Can I suggest dropping the 'are all these nice strangers going to hell' question? That's just too big for you. Can I suggest a different framework? Maybe the contribution they're willing to make for your kids is to be nice to them on the soccer field each Saturday this fall. Could you make a contribution? Could you, say, pray blessing into the lives of these nice people and dream with me of offering the wonderful Jesus to as many of them as possible? Don't do it as a way to save them from hell— that will only overwhelm and depress you. Do it, instead, as a warm-hearted gift you can offer that very few of them could offer in the same way. I think we'll both agree that knowing Jesus is the greatest, not just for churchgoers but for any human being. So … do we have a deal?"

Immediately I felt great. It was easy to pray for the people I met.

Shortly thereafter, Grace and I started hosting regular wine-and-cheese parties for these and other parents, where the adults would hang out over hors d'oeuvres while the kids, supervised by an energetic adult, played kid's games together in other parts of the house. These gatherings went really well. I think of the family visiting for the year from Japan (the dad was working, yes, at Harvard) who told us that no other Americans had invited them to their house during their year there and, realizing that Japanese people behaved the same inhospitable way towards foreigners, they were going to institute wine and cheese parties when they got home. I think of my son's coach, whom I started praying for most days just because he was so kind to my son. After one party, he asked if we could get together. He'd been sexually abused by a Boston priest as a boy and—despite on the surface seeming like one of the most confident, magnetic people in the room—his life was in crisis. He couldn't hold a job, had constant anxiety and his marriage was at risk. As a pastor, could I help him? I think of the Chilean man who'd grown up in wealth, but who'd had a breakdown after taking a fun trip to Africa on his family's money, only to get caught in Rwanda just as the genocide was breaking out. Now his life had collapsed in many ways, and he was wondering if I could do whatever pastor stuff I did that could help him in his PTSD?

You can imagine that Jesus came up, to great responsiveness and gratitude, a lot.

The question is: Is Jesus' preferred response to non-churchgoing culture to draw lines against it, pray against it, and decry its evil influence on the the lives of godly people like those in our circle? Are these guests at our wine and cheese parties the enemies of right-thinking, godly people? Or is there another option?

The Bible has a dynamic response to this question.

Most of the Old Testament has a clear take on this. Stay away from other cultures. They're horrific. They worship fertility gods. They appease their evil gods by burning up some of their kids. If you get to know them even a little bit, you'll end up intermarrying, which will bring their filth right into your godly culture. Stay away!

It's not just the early Old Testament either. Paul makes a related point in 2 Corinthians 6, in which he quotes Isaiah 52:11,

> *"Come out from them and be separate, says the Lord.*
> *Touch no unclean thing, and I will receive you."*[104]

This is a big verse, maybe even a constituting verse, for the Amish. "Be ye separate!" Have no interaction with worldly culture—which has led them into an odd alliance not with a culture from biblical times, but with 18th century Swiss German culture.[105]

Paul, whose entire ministry—entire *life*—was based upon tearing down dividing walls between his religious friends and the wider world seems to be making a specific, rather than a general, point here. Jesus was a transitional person along these lines. On the one hand, Jesus tells us he only came for his bounded-set.[106] Yet, he commissions his followers to go to the ends of the earth.[107]

He commands them to be "salt and light" to the whole world[108] to, as a friend of mine put it, "become part of the

---

104 Do I need to mention that, being Paul, he doesn't quite quote the verse that shows up there today? (This could be because he was quoting the translation called the Septuagint. We have more accurate translations today.) In Isaiah, it focuses only on the priests: "Depart, depart, go out from there!/ Touch no unclean thing!/ Come out from it and be pure,/ you who carry the articles of the Lord's house."

105 I don't think this oddity is accidental. If we "stand against" the culture of the world, we're choosing to cement ourselves into our own, quirky culture. There's no way to be culture-free.

106 Matthew 15:24

107 Matthew 28:16-20

108 Matthew 5:13-16

petri dish of culture creation." He tells parables that all point towards everyday lived life—coins, food, agriculture, animals, debt, lending, buying, parenting, planning for war, flowers, birds. Like Francis did later, Jesus sees and teaches about God in everyday life and culture. To his listeners, the images infuse the world all around them with God. The bounded-set religious people were infuriated that he was a "friend of sinners" even as he was often a critic towards these religious critics. In a religious world that regarded contact with unholiness as contaminating—one that would require the priest in the parable of the good Samaritan to walk on the other side of the road to avoid contamination from a man who might be dead—Jesus introduces the prospect that his followers, instead, would "infect" the wider world with their own health.[109] Profound fear of the world is replaced by a joyous, Franciscan journey into the heart of it in service of "being a light to the nations," the central call to God's people by the end of the Hebrew Bible.[110]

Are we called to "take back culture?"

I live in greater L.A. and I run across occasional people looking to "take Hollywood for Jesus" or to "impact culture for the gospel." You might imagine why I'd be against the first—the unaware similarities to bounded-set-edness of it. But is this chapter arguing for the second?

I don't think it is.

Think back to the image in the earlier chapter on religious squabbles. I talk there about a religious person who, rather

---

109 In Mark 8:2-3, Jesus touched a leper—which should have both exposed Jesus to this highly contagious disease and made him unclean to enter the temple. Instead things went the other way and the man no longer had leprosy.

110 Isaiah 49:6: "(God) says: 'It is too small a thing for you to be my servant to restore the tribes of Jacob and bring back those of Israel I have kept. I will also make you a light for the Gentiles, that my salvation may reach to the ends of the earth.'"

than holding truth in their hands, has instead walked inside a vast circle of truth, far bigger than they could ever traverse in their lifetimes, but which is distilled truth nonetheless. If this is the world we're in, culture is not something that can be "impacted." It's bigger than you and me. Instead, Jesus and Francis seem to encourage a joyful engagement, a happy journey in which we "let our light shine," even as we learn from all the truth around us[111] that we're so lucky to get a glimpse of.

This is a joyful rather than fearful journey, not the journey of the priest in the Good Samaritan parable, but instead the journey of Jesus and Francis. The secular cities that many of us live in are not our enemies, but offer us profound gifts and opportunities to take our place within them.

Strangely, perhaps this insight is the first step to being a centered-set revivalist.

What are the implications of this?

I can think of a few. I'm going to brazenly mix exhortations and observations.

1. Assume that every person who's ever lived wants Jesus.

If you live in a secular city, they likely don't want Christianity. They certainly don't want a theological argument. They don't want truth claims.

But they do want Jesus, and so they are not your enemies. We were created to know and love the God who made us, the same one who sent us Jesus to get an up-close picture of what he's like. All humans want that. The good news is that we don't have to be insecure! We don't have to browbeat anyone that by golly we're *right* about something! We don't have to threaten people with hell. We can be confident that, insofar as we actually know the living, communicative, loving, present Jesus, we have truly good news for everyone. We have a real contribution to make.

---

111 One of my wife's favorite truisms is "all truth is God's truth."

2. Secular culture, intriguingly, is made up of people.

This is why we don't need to take on the burden of "changing" secular culture, any more than we take on the burden of "changing" a given person. Instead, the good stuff tends to come when we *interact* with a given person, when we pray for them, when we relate to them, when we—best case— connect with them. We give and we receive. That seems to be the way relationships work best. Abstractions—or demonized, strange "outsiders"—can perhaps be "changed."[112] However, not the neighbor you and I know. They can be befriended.

Think back to the "100 arrows" idea we talked about in the centered-set chapter, the one that encouraged us that any human being can teach us things about Jesus that we need to know.

3. Genuine connection makes us joyful.

You and I have such burdens in our lives, but a universal burden-reliever is connection. When we actually connect to others—or to God or to ourselves—we tap into the one and only joy-generator that God offers us. We're relational, even us introverts. Demonizing the culture around us is disconnecting; it's against how we've been made. When the prayer leader could only demonize the abstraction he called "Harvard," he couldn't experience the joy of knowing and praying for the dedicated Harvard people I knew and loved. When we cut ourselves off from this sort of connection, we become the sort of grim, humorless, angry religious people we see on occasion in the Bible, and on occasion in religious people we meet. Francis was connected to every person he met, as well as to the whole creation. Again, the joyful revival he started lasted centuries and transformed Europe and the modern world. The stern, adversarial holiness revivals haven't pulled that off.

---

112 They can't, but they do provoke us to dream that they could!

4. Meet your neighbors.

Despite my years of pastoring, I'm not what a disinterested observer would call a friendly person. I'm, again, mildly introverted. I rarely learn the names of the baristas in the coffee shops, which I regularly work in. Pray for me.

Happily, I'm married to a woman who is much friendlier and more extroverted than I am. She does meet our neighbors and the parents of our children's friends. So, over the years, we've invited them into many different types of gatherings, from the family wine-and-cheese parties I described earlier, to seasonal open houses, to more formal "salons" in which we convene a conversation about meaning.

Here's what I've learned from this: It's fun to host the party. (A) Nobody else does it. Okay, that's an overstatement—in some places, somebody else does in fact do it. But, if you live in a secular city like mine, for the most part what you'll hear from your neighbors is that you're the first person on their block to invite them into your home. (B) If you're like me, it turns out to be more fun to host the party than to go to the (rare) party hosted by one of your neighbors. I feel awkward milling around with strangers. When I'm the host, however, I enjoy welcoming each guest and learning about them. (C) You will learn fascinating things about your neighbors. In a recent gathering, I learned that not one, but two middle-aged women there had been backup dancers in famous music videos of the 80s and 90s. Didn't see that one coming. Those neighbors you see all the time but don't actually know turn out to be really interesting people. (D) The more you do this, the more connected you will feel to your neighborhood. You'll say hi to people. They'll shout a greeting at you from across the street. They'll come running up to you to tell you they've been thinking about you. In my experience this is not the norm in the big city.

5. Pray for your six.

One more. (E) God will become part of this story. In the churches I've been a part of, we've talked about this thing we've called "praying for your six." Here's the idea. Whenever you pray for anyone—your family, anyone—also pray for your six. These are six local people who, best as you can figure out, are not experiencing much from God. They're neighbors, like I've described here. They're co-workers. A recent one for me was a supermarket checker who became friends with my daughter and me. The reason for these to be local is to connect you to your actual city, rather than only praying for your aunt in Fort Lauderdale or your old roommate who moved to Dallas.[113] Here's the thing. Maybe the reason these people might not be experiencing much from God is that no one is praying for them! Maybe you can be that agent of God for them! That dynamic coach of my son who pulled me aside to talk about being abused by a priest? One of my six. That Chilean man with PTSD who asked me to help him find God again? One of my six.

Here's my unprovable belief: God honors people and churches who pray for their six. He entrusts them with awesome things they couldn't otherwise experience. All because they notice the people they rub shoulders with daily. Rather than cursing their faceless, "godless" city, they bless hundreds and hundreds of non-churchgoing inhabitants of that city.

6. Be the culture creator that you are.

I love the upshot of Andy Crouch's book *Culture Making* in which he argues that all of us can and should create stuff. We can make the garden that brings beauty to our block. We can write the poems that some of our friends read and enjoy. We can write the memoir so our kids can know who we really are and a bit about their ancestors. We can create. Maybe we swing for the fences and write that feature film or novel, or we pitch that new TV series. I know churchgoers doing that. Now, true, most of us who swing away like that don't connect. By definition, only very few people get to be the one-in-a-million cultural icon. But, in Crouch's world, why not take your swing?

---

113 By all means, pray for those people too.

In this world, we're creating not out of the burden to "change culture." If that's our view, we need to get over ourselves. Instead we do it for the Franciscan joy of it. Francis didn't sing to the birds in hopes of landing a Billboard-charting hit song. Grace composes little ditties about God that we've sung to our kids at bedtime. Her songs are really good! When our oldest was two, she wrote her first chart-topper, which Grace would sing to him as he put a plush-toy ball through a hoop for hours: "Benjamin Loves Basketball." Pretty darn infectious. Most likely, you'll never hear it.

7. **Or just engage the larger culture in any way that comes to mind.**

Just do it as a joyful Franciscan, rather than as a stern holiness preacher.

How does this interact with our hope of changing the world?

My circle, maybe like your circle, is full of awesome people who are trying to address some horrible things in our world. They're trying to end sex slavery in their city, or in the world at large. They're fighting racism or sexism. They're engaged, caring people. What we're talking about here would, I hope, only cheer them on in their great work.

What this chapter is talking about, though, would add the texture that, as we fight the evils in our world, we also joyfully engage with the actual city around us rather than "standing against it." It would also recognize that "changing our world" wholesale might be a step beyond what's helpful for us to dream for. The Hero's Journey, for instance, is funny in this respect. In it, you're on a journey to *save* the world—but that turns out to be a different and bigger thing than "changing" it. Initially, the Shire has no idea what Frodo and Sam and their friends have done on its behalf.

Whether we get the satisfaction of things-will-never-be-the-same "changing" our world, we're promised that we do get the joyful opportunity to do our part as we live in our world.

As we find joy from connecting with God, people, ourselves, our city and our world, we get to play a relational role in everything we touch, which does seem like a big deal. Like Francis, we get to pray for the people we connect with and for our world—even as we delight in Jesus and as we share honestly and reciprocally with our neighbors. We might start centered-set communities of faith.

Now that I think about it, Francis and his followers did profoundly change the world. Maybe to a greater degree than any other group of people—at least who changed the world for good, not evil—have ever pulled off. But, like Frodo, Francis's goals weren't actually to change his world. He was focused on Jesus. It's been the disapproving revolutionaries, the Lenins, who've been the change-the-world types.

I, again, am a revivalist. I'm not sure if the exact model of the Franciscans would work as our tactic. They would spend half their time in prayer and the other half preaching about the goodness of Jesus in new town squares. (They particularly enjoyed provoking hostile reactions.) They made their living by begging, but they did, in their day, hold up the always-good Jesus like the snake on the stick and watched as he drew people to himself.

Whatever it turns out to look like, I nonetheless want to take my place in a centered-set revival for Jesus that will sweep the world.

To my mind, the Franciscan—or, better stated, the "Jesus"—plan is our best bet to pull that off.

8

If You Have a Moment, Let's Kick Off a New Jesus Movement

The best part about knowing God.

I'VE FIGURED IT all out. I'm pretty excited.

The best part about knowing God is … I mean, I feel a little dorky saying it … it's knowing God.

The best part is not "being biblical." It's not even answered prayer, as great as it is to get answered prayer. It's not caring for poor people in your or my community, as worthy as that is. It's not "being relevant" to culture. It's not even the friends we make in a church. I mean, heck, it's not even going to heaven when we die. Those, again, are all great things; they just aren't the best thing.

The best part about knowing God is knowing God. It's really great to know God. Everything else flows from this.

We get plenty of encouragements along this line in the Bible. Hebrews 4 rhapsodizes about how we're crazy if we don't take God up on his offer to "enter into Sabbath rest." It's as if there's a kind of "God Zone" which we're sternly advised to walk into day in and day out, moment in and moment out, one in which we'll discover why we're alive on earth. Earlier, Jesus says if we pull off this thing called being "poor in spirit," we get this amazing thing called "the kingdom of heaven"— the God Zone! When Moses found his groove with God, God started showing up in a thick cloud.

This is a big part of the promise of the Second Naiveté. Being human and all, we'll walk around the whole fallen world and have heartaches and triumphs and confusing times and betrayals and beautiful sunset dinners and health crises. But if we do this while actually knowing God, we'll walk our journey in the presence of the living Jesus who loves us, talks with us, encourages us and guides us.

This is such a big deal.

Grace and I host a Bible discussion each week. At the last one, we talked about the Beatitudes. A bright, 12-year-old girl was not happy. "So this is telling me that if I just accept having a terrible life—being poor in spirit and persecuted and meek— that I'll get to go to heaven when I die? I already have enough troubles with self-image—I don't think I'm cool or pretty or popular and I worry that my life isn't going anywhere and no one will want me. If Jesus is saying that I just need to accept that everything will be crappy and it will pay off for me so far in the future that I can't even really keep it in mind, then no thanks on my end." Welcome to the Bible discussions in our house.

After a respectful pause, one of the adults offered another possibility. "You know that everyone in this room thinks you're beautiful, smart, talented and awesome and have a brighter future than any of us. But, be that as it may, I think the offer of this passage is really different than you seem to see it. I think it's saying that, however you're feeling at any given point, however unhappy or happy, your life will go a lot better if you do it with God. You'll get this thing called the kingdom of heaven, which evidently is something people have wanted for millennia."

"So," she said, "you're saying that, if I'm going to suck, I should suck with God and then maybe I'll get something good."

"Not exactly how I'd phrase it," the adult said. "But, yes, I think so."

The girl thought about this for a moment and then asked us if we'd heard about Hegel, whom she'd recently learned about. According to her, Hegel suggested that we start off with an idea called a "thesis." Then we go to the opposite of the idea, called an "antithesis." Finally, as those two opposite things work together for a bit, we get a third thing, the good thing, called a "synthesis." "So," she said, "is this like that? The thesis, again, is that I suck and my life sucks. The antithesis is that God is awesome and loves me and invites me into some kind of God Zone with him. And the synthesis is somehow that I get a kind of life as the actual, perhaps sucky me which is really awesome and is better than if I'd never sucked in the first place?" None of us were Hegel experts, but that sounded right to us.

What non-churchgoers want.

In Cambridge, I'd go so far as to say that this girl's insight was the secret of our success. What we discovered local non-churchgoers wanted wasn't some kind of moral teaching, or Bible instruction or even good self-help tools like positive thinking. As much as they might cheer it on, they didn't in the first instance want a chance to help poor people. They didn't even want a new pool of friends.

They wanted God.

It seems pretty straightforward, though I can't tell you how many pastors I've talked to for whom this is befuddling. These pastors understand that these non-churchgoers might, say, need to convert or risk hell. However, the idea of just directing these people towards the interactive God who will very much be there for them is not obvious to them. In that sense, the secret of our success was being centered-set.

Let's call the question. Do you buy that it's all about connection? Is the fundamental cry of every heart to connect? Is this a bigger need than "being right" about something (like God or politics or morality)? Are you sold that the connection that God is offering us is the road to other great things, like connection to others and, per the last chapter, to our cities? Does it hit you at a heart level that what everyone you ever meet wants most is that thing Paul describes as the greatest of Jesus' miracles—"breaking dividing walls," forging a fundamental connection instead of being consigned to ongoing division, alienation, loneliness and carrying the full weight of the pressures of our lives? Are you eager for Jesus' gift of connecting you to yourself, past all the negative self-talk and anxiety to the rich hope of childlike faith on the road to the second naiveté?

Once people get a taste for this, it's hard to go back.

I've now gotten to know hundreds of non-churchgoers who've found their way to faith in God on just these terms. When they need to move to other cities, they often ask where they can find another church like this. They'd never known such congregations existed! Now they can't imagine any other kind.

What's been interesting to me, as I press them to tell me concretely what they're hoping for, is that they're on the lookout for what, at first blush, might seem like five surface-level characteristics.

They tell me their hoped-for church would be:

- Alive in Jesus.

These friends are not looking for less focus on Jesus, but more. They want lively worship and faith and prayer and miracles. They're supernaturalists, rather than being skeptical secularists. Again, what they most want is God.

- Diverse.

Once they leave home, most people live in a diverse world. Colleges are almost all quite ethnically diverse, as are most large workforces. Among institutions, churches are often the only mono-ethnic holdouts. This seems creepy and disconnected to my crew.

- Inclusive.

It baffles my friends why anyone who earnestly wants to follow Jesus would be denied the opportunity to do so on the same terms as everyone else. The rapid inclusion of LGBTQ people as full partners in America is mirrored in my would-be-churchgoing circle.

•   Politically nuanced.

It's not that my friends don't have their own, often strong political opinions. But, as we've talked about, they recognize that politics increasingly involves demonizing opponents, rather than earnestly working to create a just and thriving country. When churches participate in this demonization—even if they do it from my friend's own political perspectives!—my friends head for the door.[114] Again, they're sold that Jesus' work is to break dividing walls, not reinforce them.

•   Attractive and comprehensible to outsiders.

These friends seem to be natural evangelists. They want a church to invite other non-churchgoing friends to, but they commonly tell me that the churches they visit, whatever their other challenges, would repel and baffle their friends.

What do you think of those five characteristics? I'm not sure that each of the six distinctives are encapsulated there, but maybe you can see how they bring some power as a

---

114 One friend, hearing this, strongly wants me to talk about a positive political agenda—at the very least about justice and caring for the poor. "Yes," he says, "the sort of nuance you're talking about is absolutely important. But don't you want to be *about* something politically? Are you telling me that the people you're talking to *wouldn't* want a church that cares about these things?" Clearly, he has a compelling point. In fact, every church I work with does have a concrete focus on justice and the poor, so his point stands even if only based on the facts. However, the five-fold church my friends describe isn't meant to be a fully-orbed church. It's more like a super-unusual starting point. It's a baseline from which a church can grow rather than a church itself. These five points are low-bar.

starting point, how centered-set is all but required to be both "alive in Jesus" *and* "inclusive," and how it works for diversity in a way that bounded-set couldn't.

Why not a new Jesus movement?

I had my encounter with Jesus right at the tail end of what might be the western world's last revival: the Jesus Movement. Jesus People were hippies who, in the middle of their tuning in to higher consciousness, found themselves tuning to Jesus. I pastored in a group of churches that formed as the Jesus Movement was winding down. The first of these churches met on an Orange County beach with a thousand young, counter-culture kids attending. That first pastor is a friend, and he tells inspiring stories of dozens of strangers converting to Jesus through him each day. Every. Single. Day. He tells me that, in those days, he'd be ashamed to get on a plane and get off without having led someone to faith in Jesus. I love inspiring books from this era that are right along these lines like Merlin Carothers's *Prison to Praise* or Floyd McClung's *Living on the Devil's Doorstep.* They make the reader want to plunge into the adventure of life with Jesus.

Yet, I know some of these authors as well. Like my friend who led the services on the beach, they tell me that that era is very much over. The flow of conversions they saw has slowed or ended, and the vibrancy of the hippie, change-the-world ethic of the Jesus Movement largely turned into what would seem like its opposite; these were the people who fueled the religious right. When their overflowing faith that Jesus was going to usher in a new world faded, did they channel that same enthusiasm into looking for political leaders to do the ushering? Not long ago I talked with a prominent anthropologist who asked me for leads in exploring her next project—why, she asked me, did the vast majority of Jesus People converts go from being cutoff-wearing hippies to being fundamentalists? I think it's that many of the hippie converts entered faith from Stage 1—from drug addiction and free sex (and STDs) and living on the streets—and so Stage 2 offered lifelines to drowning people. Many of these people were so grateful for their rescue that they couldn't move past the unyielding structure that Stage 2 gave them, and so they became hard Stage 2.

But my revivalist core has kicked in again. My family and I traded in pastoring a thriving, prominent church in hope of seeing something bigger and more-far-reaching than that.

Why can't we all dream for a new, Franciscan, Jesus Movement?

I mean, we'd seem to have a few things going for us.

First, the starting point is embarrassingly easy. All it takes is pointing people to Jesus, to the one who, like the snake on the stick, will call anyone who looks his way to himself. Now the challenge, of course, is to unlearn all the dross that's offered itself as a substitute for this. It's hard to unlearn all of our moralisms and "biblical worldviews" and correct voting choices and bounded-set-edness! It can feel disorienting to even consider what would replace those things! However, if they've set themselves up as a substitute for Franciscan trust in the living, communicating, loving, life-changing Jesus, it should be a fun unlearning. Offering still more upside, these moralisms—and the us/them focus that accompanies them—have been blamed in good part for the horrendous rate of youth-group kids who leave faith. So we might just regain our own children for faith in Jesus. After all, they too want connection.

The second step would also seem obvious and easy until we realize how rare it's become. Invite everyone into this connection with Jesus. Point everyone towards Jesus, towards our "snake on a stick."

Everyone.

Again, it may seem obvious, but it turns out that we church people have become addicted to making clear who the good and bad people are, which has made us forget how to do this inviting. This is why the low-bar quality of the five

characteristics seems so helpful to me. To review: Alive in
Jesus. Diverse. Inclusive. Politically nuanced. Attractive and
comprehensible to outsiders.

Think about your own city. How many churches do you
know of that would fit this description? In most cities, the
answer is very few to none. Would you dream with me for
more where that came from?

Let Jesus do the work.

It seems to me that we're throwing away a pretty darn
powerful resource when we don't approach church this way.
Jesus! As Francis found to be true, Jesus promises that, if we
point people towards him, *he'll* do the work! He'll devote all
his power as God to draw all people to himself. It makes me
feel bad when I content myself with moralisms and us/them
and quoting my favorite scholars when all the power of the
living God is offered to me.

It's also almost irresistible for church people to trade this
power for a very-related-but-actually-kind-of-opposite thing:
church growth. Think back to our discussion of tactics. Now,
just to say, I love large churches! I ran a very large church
myself and wouldn't have traded it for a smaller church! But,
the tactics of church growth are, at best, necessary but not
sufficient to what we're talking about here and are, at worst, a
substitute for them. This new Jesus movement would require
a kind of Franciscan, joyful indifference to growth as it walked
out into the hero's journey of faith in hopes of offering the
living Jesus to as many people as possible. By all accounts,
Francis had no church growth plan when we went out to
rebuild the church that was outside of town. The power of
the Azusa Street revival was not its tactics, but its faith—its
multiracial prayer for God to come with great power and joy.

Blue Ocean churches each want to be good, competent
churches. They want to learn from one another and from
anyone else about how to be responsible, thoughtful
congregational leaders. In their eagerness to experience the

living God themselves and to point others his way, they've embraced being big or being small. Some of these churches have realized that, while they embodied four of the five key characteristics, they weren't fully inclusive, so they rectified that. Often this was at the cost of losing (usually angrily) their most conservative members, who were most of their biggest givers and who sometimes rallied other conservative big givers to leave with them. But these Blue Ocean leaders realized the power of passages like Hebrews 10:

> *"But recall those earlier days when, after you had been enlightened, you endured a hard struggle with sufferings, sometimes being publicly exposed to abuse and persecution, and sometimes being partners with those so treated. For … you cheerfully accepted the plundering of your possessions, knowing that you yourselves possessed something better and more lasting. Do not, therefore, abandon that confidence of yours; it brings a great reward."*

Walking out into the world on the great adventure of faith, hoping to experience Jesus yourself as you fight the fight of faith daily, and also hoping to point others Jesus' way—this is just the greatest. It addresses questions of what your life is about. It invites creativity and experimentation because there's no possibility of failing. My friends in this endeavor have taken in great business advice like: Try fast. Fail fast. Evaluate fast. Try again fast. They've seen approaches that have worked wonderfully suddenly quit working, and so have realized that constant innovation is going to be the watchword of the rest of their lives. The nature of constant innovation is that many new things don't work, but as we keep at it, we see wonderful things. All in company of the very much alive, very much communicative, very encouraging Jesus.

Three days ago, I was picking up my young daughter at her new friend's house and I was talking to this girl's parents. They were inquisitive people and so right away we were talking

about my atheist starting point and the kind of churches I
was working with and why I'd been so helped by Jesus. The
husband was secular Jewish and the wife, a Jewish convert,
had grown up Unitarian. "Wow," the husband said after we'd
talked for half an hour. "Why haven't I heard about this?" The
wife interjected, "Why hasn't *everyone* heard about this?"

American public life strikes most Americans as deeply
broken, if Congress's 9% approval rating is any indication.
Red states and blue states are increasingly siloed off from
one another. Bounded-set can't address this. Who knows the
virtuous cycle that could come from a new, centered-set Jesus
movement?

Clearly we might not get this. Very few people have kicked
off three-century-long revivals that also transformed their
larger worlds, as Francis and his friends did.

But, I mean, what are you doing these days? Are you up to
something that sounds like *more* fun than this?

Epilogue: You Want More Resources? We've Got More Resources.

IF THIS VIEW of the world grabs you, join me and my co-hosts for our weekly *Blue Ocean World* podcast. We'll talk through current events, bring up the big questions of God or meaning that are on our minds, and introduce you to fascinating guests (as I write this, recent guests have been Walter "Robby" Robinson—Michael Keaton played him in *Spotlight*—and Brian McLaren and *New York Times* journalists and renowned academics). You can find it on iTunes or at hellohoratio.com.

The Blue Ocean Faith website at blueoceanfaith.org would also be worth your exploration. Along with highlighting congregations pursuing this, it's full of resources like the Blue Ocean Churches manual I mentioned and the Seek class and the yearly, Lenten Leaps of Faith that churches all over the country look forward to. I also publish regular thought pieces there. (Key sections of this book got worked out in that forum.)

You could meet fellow explorers at our yearly Blue Ocean Summit (details on the Blue Ocean Faith website) or at periodic regional conferences.

We host periodic cohorts for pastors who are looking for more connection and training around this approach to church along with periodic webinars. You can contact us through the website to let us know about your interest.

To a new Jesus Movement!

Appendix: Works Cited

Bonhoeffer, Dietrich, *The Cost of Discipleship* (Macmillan, 1963).

Brother Lawrence, *The Practice of the Presence of God*.

Campbell, Joseph, *The Hero with a Thousand Faces* (New World Library, 2008).

Carothers, Merlin R., *Prison to Praise* (Carothers, 1970)

Chesterton, G.K., *Orthodoxy*.

Chesterton, G.K., *St. Francis of Assisi*.

Cox, Harvey, *The Future of Faith* (HarperOne, 2010)

Crouch, Andy, *Culture Making: Recovering Our Creative Calling* (IVP, 2013).

Dillenberger, John, *Martin Luther: Selections from His Writings* (Doubleday, 1961).

Edwards, Jonathan, *The Works of Jonathan Edwards, 2 Volumes* (Hendrickson, 1993).

Emerson, Michael O. and Smith, Christian, *Divided by Faith: Evangelical Religion and the Problem of Race in America* (Oxford, 2001).

Enns, Peter, *The Bible Tells Me So: Why Defending Scripture Has Made Us Unable to Read It* (HarperOne, 2015).

Fuller, Daniel P., *The Unity of the Bible: Unfolding God's Plan for Humanity* (Zondervan, 2000).

Grubb, Norman, *Rees Howells: Intercessor* (CLC, 1998).

Hiebert, Paul G., *Anthropological Reflections on Missiological Issues* (Baker Academic, 1994).

McClung, Floyd, *Living on the Devil's Doorstep: From Kabul to Amsterdam* (YWAM, 1999).

Nelson, John, *The Little Way of Saint Therese of Lisieux: Into the Arms of Love* (Liguori, 1998).

Olson, Roger E., *Reformed and Always Reforming: The Postconservative Approach to Evangelical Theology* (Baker Academic, 2007).

Peck, M. Scott, *Further Along the Road Less Traveled: The Unending Journey Towards Spiritual Growth* (Touchstone, 1993).

Peck, M. Scott, *The Road Less Traveled: A New Psychology of Love, Traditional Values and Spiritual Growth* (Touchstone, 2003).

Putnam, Robert D. and Campbell, David E., *American Grace: How Religion Divides and Unites Us* (Simon & Schuster, 2012).

Sacks, Jonathan, *Not in God's Name: Confronting Religious Violence* (Schrocken, 2015).

Schmelzer, Dave, *Blue Ocean Churches: Thriving Congregations in a Changing World* (blueoceanfaith.org, 2010).

Schmelzer, Dave, *Not the Religious Type: Confessions of a Turncoat Atheist* (Tyndale, 2008).

Tickle, Phyllis, *The Great Emergence: How Christianity is Changing and Why* (Baker, 2008).

Vaillant, George E., *Triumph of Experience: The Men of the Harvard Grant Study* (Belknap, 2015).

Vogler, Christopher, *The Writer's Journey: Mythic Structure for Writers* (Michael Wiese, 2007).

Wicker, Christine, *The Fall of the Evangelical Nation: The Surprising Crisis Inside the Church* (HarperOne, 2008).

Wilson, Ken, *A Letter to My Congregation: An evangelical pastor's path to embracing people who are gay, lesbian and transgender into the company of Jesus* (David Crumm, 2014).

Yancey, George, *One Body One Spirit: Principles of Successful Multiracial Churches* (IVP, 2003).

CPSIA information can be obtained
at www.ICGtesting.com
Printed in the USA
LVOW12s2314110517
534233LV00001B/97/P